Essential Histories

# The French Religious Wars 1562–1598

Essential Histories

# The French Religious Wars 1562–1598

Robert J Knecht

First published in Great Britain in 2002 by Osprey Publishing,
Elms Court, Chapel Way, Botley, Oxford OX2 9LP, UK
Email: info@ospreypublishing.com

ISBN 1 84176 395 0

Editor: Rebecca Cullen
Design: Ken Vail Graphic Design, Cambridge, UK
Cartography by The Map Studio
Index by Robert J Knecht
Picture research by Image Select International
Origination by Grasmere Digital Imaging, Leeds, UK
Printed and bound in China by L. Rex Printing Company Ltd.

02 03 04 05 06   10 9 8 7 6 5 4 3 2 1

For a complete list of titles available from Osprey Publishing
please contact:

Osprey Direct UK, PO Box 140,
Wellingborough, Northants, NN8 2FA, UK
Email: info@ospreydirect.co.uk

Osprey Direct USA, c/o MBI Publishing,
PO Box 1, 729 Prospect Ave
Osceola, WI 54020, USA.
Email: info@ospreydirectusa.com

**www.ospreypublishing.com**

# Contents

# Introduction

At the beginning of the 16th century France was among the most powerful kingdoms in western Europe. By the end, it had become perhaps the weakest. The reason for this collapse was the long series of civil wars, commonly known as the French Wars of Religion, which erupted in 1562 and lasted intermittently until 1598.

France in 1515 was not yet a fully-developed nation state. She still lacked well-defined frontiers, a common language and a unified legal system. The kingdom was smaller than modern France and contained three foreign enclaves: Calais, the Comtat-Venaissin and the principality of Orange. The duchies of Brittany and Lorraine and the small kingdom of Navarre in the south remained independent. Alsace was still part of the Holy Roman Empire. Roads were few in number and poor, and river traffic was impeded by numerous tolls. Travel was therefore slow by modern standards. The journey from Paris to Amiens normally took two days, from Paris to Bordeaux seven and a half, from Paris to Lyon six to eight and from Paris to Marseille 10 to 14.

In 1515 France was relatively prosperous. Outbreaks of plague were fewer and less widespread than in the past and no grain famine occurred between 1440 and 1520. The population probably doubled from 1450 to 1560, when it may have reached 16 million. The need to feed more mouths stimulated agricultural production, though this was achieved by land clearance and reclamation rather than improved farming techniques. The rise in population was reflected in the growth of towns. Paris had a population of around 300,000 in 1565. After Paris came four provincial towns (Rouen, Lyon, Toulouse and Orleans) of between 40,000 and 70,000 inhabitants, then a score of between 10,000 and 30,000, then another 40 or so of between 5,000 and 10,000. Many towns had fewer than 5,000 inhabitants. The character of each was determined by its main activity. Trade was important to all of them, but some were administrative, intellectual and ecclesiastical centres as well. Most were protected by walls. Underlying the growth of towns was an economic boom that lasted from about 1460 to 1520. France was largely self-sufficient in basic necessities, like grain, wine, salt and textiles. Cloth-making was the most important industry, but printing was becoming important. The vast majority of the people were peasants who lived in France's 30,000 villages. Each village had its social hierarchy headed by a *seigneur*, who was usually but not always a nobleman (a *seigneurie* could be purchased). A *seigneurie* was a landed estate of variable size, divided into two parts: firstly the demesne, including the *seigneur's* house and tribunal (he had judicial rights over his tenants) and the lands and woods which he cultivated himself; and secondly the lands entrusted to peasants, who cultivated them more or less freely in return for various dues.

Contemporaries divided urban society into two groups: the rich (*aisés*) and the proletariat (*menu peuple*), but the reality was more complex. Apart from the nobility and clergy, which were not exclusively urban categories, the upper end of urban society included merchants and office-holders. The core consisted of artisans and small to middling merchants. Below them were the manual workers, including journeymen paid in money or kind.

France was governed by a king who was 'absolute' in that he was responsible only to God. Women were debarred from the throne by the Salic law, one of the so-called 'fundamental laws' which the king was supposed to uphold. He succeeded to the throne from the instant of his predecessor's death. His coronation was no longer considered essential to the exercise of kingship, but remained important as a symbol of the close alliance between church and state. The king took an oath to defend the church and to root out heresy from his dominions, and the anointing gave him a semi-priestly character. He bore the title of 'Most Christian King', and was believed to be able to heal the sick. The king governed with the advice of a council, though he always had the final say. Legislation was framed by the chancery headed by the Chancellor of France, who was invariably a jurist and often a churchman. It was the nearest equivalent to a modern ministry, with a staff of 120 in 1500 which grew larger during the 16th century. Other senior ministers included the Grand Master, who held sway over the court, and the Constable of France, who commanded the army in the king's absence. The court comprised the king's household and those of his family as well as a crowd of hangers-on. It could number as many as 10,000 people, yet it remained nomadic until the end of the century. Except in winter, when the roads were bad, the court travelled incessantly. In an age of growing political centralisation the king needed to show himself to his subjects.

The basic unit of local government was the *bailliage* (sometimes called *sénéchaussée*) of which there were about 100 varying greatly in size. The tribunal of the *bailliage* judged cases on appeal from inferior courts and crimes committed against the crown. It also had important administrative powers. Above the *bailliages* were the *parlements* of which there were seven in 1500 (Paris, Toulouse, Grenoble, Bordeaux, Dijon, Rouen and Aix-en-Provence). The oldest and most prestigious was the Parlement of Paris. Though fixed in Paris, its jurisdiction covered two-thirds of the kingdom. Unlike the English Parliament, it was not a representative body, but the highest court of law under the king. Even so, it had

important administrative responsibilities, including the ratification of royal legislation. A law could only become enforceable after registration by the Parlement.

A major figure in local government was the provincial governor. There were 11 governorships (*gouvernements*), corresponding roughly with the kingdom's border provinces. Governors were normally princes of the blood or high-ranking nobles. A governor's attendance at court gave him unique opportunities of patronage which he might use to build up a powerful clientèle within his province. Nearly all governors were captains of the *gendarmerie*, the heavy armoured cavalry, which was the only standing army. They controlled recruitment and promotion within its ranks. The most complex and least efficient part of French government was the fiscal administration. This was built up around two kinds of revenue: the 'ordinary' revenue, which the king drew from his domain, and the 'extraordinary' revenue which he got from taxation. The latter comprised three main taxes: the *taille*, the *gabelle* (salt tax) and the *aides*. The *taille* was the only direct tax. It was levied annually, the amount being decided by the king's council.

The French monarchy was not strong enough to ignore the traditional rights and privileges of its subjects. The standing army of around 25,000 men in peacetime could not hold down a population of 16 million, and the royal civil service was minute by modern standards. The monarchy needed to enlist the co-operation of its subjects, and one way it could do this was by using representative institutions. At the national level the Estates-General were made up of representatives of the three estates: clergy, nobility and third estate, but the king was not obliged to call them. They did not meet between 1484 and 1560. However, a number of French provinces, known as *pays d'états*, continued to have estates of their own. Meeting usually once a year, they apportioned and collected royal taxes, raised troops, repaired fortifications, built hospitals and engaged in poor relief.

# Chronology

1559  **April**  Peace of Cateau-Cambrésis
**July**  Death of King Henry II
1560  **March**  Edict of Amboise
**March**  Tumult of Amboise
**May**  Edict of Romorantin
**December**  Death of King Francis II,
regency of Catherine de Medici
**December**  Estates-General of Orleans
1561  **January**  Ordinance of Orleans
**September–October**  Colloquy
of Poissy
1562  **January**  Edict of Saint-Germain,
also called Edict of January
**March**  Massacre of Wassy
**December**  Battle of Dreux
1563  **February**  François, second duc de
Guise assassinated
**March**  Edict of Amboise
**August**  Majority of King Charles IX
declared at Rouen
1564  Start of Charles IX's 'Grand tour'
of France
**April**  Anglo-French treaty of Troyes
**June**  Bayonne interview between
Catherine de Medici and duke of Alba
1566  Henri, duc d'Orléans becomes duc
d'Anjou and his brother
François becomes duc d'Alençon.
**May**  End of Charles IX's 'Grand tour'
**August**  Dutch revolt begins
1567  **September**  'Surprise de Meaux'
**November**  Battle of Saint-Denis; death
of Constable Anne de Montmorency
1568  **March**  Peace of Longjumeau
**May**  Fall from power of the
Chancellor, Michel de l'Hospital
**August**  Start of third religious war
1569  **March**  Battle of Jarnac; murder
of Louis, prince de Condé
**June**  Skirmish at La Roche-l'Abeille
**October**  Battle of Moncontour
**October–December**  Siege and fall
of Saint-Jean d'Angély

1570  Retreat of Coligny from the south-west
to the Loire
**June**  Battle of Arnay-le-Duc
**August**  Peace and Edict of
Saint-Germain
1571  **October**  Battle of Lepanto
**December**  Riot following the removal
of the cross of Gastines in Paris
1572  **April**  Capture of Brill by Dutch
Sea-Beggars
**July**  Defeat of Genlis outside Mons
**August**  Massacre of St Bartholomew's
Day; murder of Admiral Coligny
**October**  Start of fourth war
**December**  Siege of La Rochelle begins
1573  **May**  Henri duc d'Anjou elected king
of Poland
**July**  Siege of La Rochelle lifted
**July**  Edict of Boulogne ends fourth war
**December**  Henri d'Anjou leaves
France for Poland
**December**  Huguenot assembly
at Millau organises resistance
1574  **May**  Death of King Charles IX
**September**  Rebellion of
Montmorency-Damville
**September**  Henry III returns
from Poland
1575  **January**  Alliance between
Montmorency-Damville and Huguenots
**February**  Coronation and marriage
of Henry III
**September**  Flight of duc d'Alençon
from court
**October**  Battle of Dormans
**November**  Truce of Champigny-sur-
Veude
1576  **February**  Flight of Henri de Navarre
from court
**May**  Edict of Beaulieu also called
'Peace of Monsieur'
**May**  First League formed at Péronne
**December**  Estates-General meet at Blois

1577    **February** Closure of Estates-General
**May** Sack of La Charité-sur-Loire
by Anjou
**May** Sack of Issoire by Anjou
**September** Peace of Bergerac
**September** Edict of Poitiers

1578    **February** Anjou's second escape from
court
**October** Catherine de Medici's peace
mission to the Midi
**December** Anjou fails to capture
Mons

1579    **February** Catherine de' Medici and
king of Navarre meet at Nérac
**February** Treaty of Nérac
**August** Anjou captures Cambrai

1580    **April–May** The Lovers' War
in the Midi
**May** Siege and capture of Cahors by
Henri de Navarre
**November** Peace of Fleix

1581    **September** Marriage of Anne de
Joyeuse and Henry III's sister-in-law,
Marguerite de Lorraine

1582    **February** The duc d'Anjou's second
expedition to the Low Countries

1583    **January** Anjou fails to capture
Antwerp
**November** Assembly of Notables
at Saint-Germain-en-Laye

1584    **June** Death of the duc d'Anjou
**September** Formation of the second
League at Nancy
**December** Treaty of Joinville
between League and Philip II of Spain

1585    **March** Manifesto of Péronne
**July** Treaty of Nemours between
Henry III and the League
**August** New alliance between
Henri de Navarre and
Montmorency-Damville
**September** Pope Sixtus V deprives
Navarre and Condé of their rights to
the French throne

1586    **August** Talks between Catherine de'
Medici and Henri de Navarre at Saint-
Brice

1587    **July** Joint declaration of Navarre,
Condé and Montmorency-Damville
**October** Battle of Coutras

**October** Battle of Vimory
**November** Battle of Auneau

1588    **March** Death of Henri de Condé
at Saint-Jean d'Angély
**May** Day of the Barricades
**July** Edict of Union
**October** Estates-General meet at Blois
**December** Assassination of Henri duc
de Guise and his brother, cardinal
Louis de Guise

1589    **January** Death of Catherine
de' Medici
**January** Closure of the
Estates-General
**February** General council of the
Union set up
**April** Treaty of Tours between
Henry III and Henri de Navarre
**May–June** Siege of Paris
**May** Sixtus V excommunicates
and deposes Henry III
**August** Henry III assassinated
**September** Battle of Arques

1590    **March** Battle of Ivry
**May–September** Siege of Paris
by Henry IV

1591    **November** Execution of President
Brisson

1592    **April** Alexander of Parma relieves
Rouen

1593    **January–July** Estates of the League
meet in Paris
**July** Conversion of Henry IV

1594    **February** Henry IV crowned
at Chartres
**March** Paris falls to Henry IV

1595    **January** Henry IV declares war
on Spain
**June** Skirmish at Fontaine-Française
**September** Henry IV absolved by
the pope

1596    Treaty of Folembray with duc de
Mayenne
Fall of La Fère
**January** Assembly of Notables
at Rouen

1597    **March** Amiens captured
Surrender of the League in Brittany

1598    **April** Edict of Nantes
**May** Peace of Vervins

# Religious dissent and aristocratic discontent

The series of civil wars which tore France apart between 1562 and 1598 are commonly called the Wars of Religion, but it has been suggested that religion was used by the nobles who fought in the wars as a cloak of respectability for their own selfish aims. The nobility certainly played a key role in the wars, and their motives need to be considered. Wealth was not the only criterion distinguishing them from commoners – they also enjoyed a number of legal and customary privileges, including exemption from direct taxation. There were broadly two kinds of nobles in France: nobles 'of the sword' who had won their spurs by fighting, and nobles 'of the robe' who acquired their status by owning an office. To be accepted as noble, a person needed a family line stretching back beyond living memory. A particular style of life was also essential. A nobleman could not dabble in mundane occupations, like shop-keeping or a craft trade. He needed leisure to exercise body and mind. For a long time proof of nobility rested on the open testimony of the elders in a community. They would focus on the battles in which a nobleman had fought and on the frontal wounds he had received. Death in battle was the supreme justification of nobility. From the sixteenth century onwards the crown demanded written proofs of nobility, yet the nobility was not a closed caste. It could be entered in various ways: a man might do all the things expected of a nobleman hoping that in time he would be accepted as such. He might be ennobled by the king or might acquire an office that carried noble status.

Contemporaries identified nobility with virtue. This was commonly equated with military virtue, consisting of courage, endurance, mental and visual alertness, and a desire to acquire fame. The creation of units of heavy armoured cavalry, called *compagnies d'ordonnance* (in the late 15th century) offered the nobility opportunities for military service. They also reinforced the notion that war was the ideal way of life for a nobleman, and the Italian Wars which began in 1494 offered noblemen chances to show off their virtue. But the nobility also claimed the right to exercise the highest functions of state, and those who embraced a military career were never more than a minority – the majority preferred to live peacefully on their estates.

Charles cardinal of Lorraine (1525–1574). He and his elder brother, François, second duc de Guise, shared power under the young king Francis II. Although the cardinal toyed with the idea of reaching a religious compromise with the German Lutherans, most Huguenots regarded him as their main persecutor. (Musée Condé Chantilly, Giraudon)

François de Lorraine, 2nd duc de Guise (1519-1563). Related by marriage to the King, he and his brother, Charles, cardinal of Lorraine, virtually seized control of the government during the brief reign of Francis II. François de Guise became a national hero after successfully defending Metz against the Emperor Charles V in 1553 and capturing Calais from the English in 1558. But in March 1562 he presided over the massacre of a Huguenot congregation at Wassy, which may be regarded as the opening shot in the Wars of Religion. He was besieging Orleans in October 1563 when he was murdered by Poltrot de Mere, a Protestant nobleman. A bitter vendetta ensued between the duke's heirs and Admiral Coligny whom they accussed of instigating the murder. (Musée Condé Chantilly, Giraudon)

At the top of the aristocratic pyramid were some 20 families, who were pre-eminent on account of their landed wealth, the importance of their offices and the extent of their family ties. They included the 'princes of the blood', who were all legitimate male descendants of Hugh Capet (987–996) – but also the descendants of King Louis IX, and the so-called 'foreign princes'. The Valois were the ruling dynasty. Closely related to them were the Bourbons, who were descended from Robert, the son of Louis IX. Their head was Antoine, king of Navarre. The 'foreign princes' were naturalised Frenchmen who traced their family origins to a foreign country, the most famous being the Guises, a younger branch of the ruling house of Lorraine. Its founder, Claude de Guise, the first duke, became related by marriage to the French royal family. His six sons all became distinguished soldiers or churchmen. François, the second duke, was a fine soldier who captured Calais from the English in 1558. He married Anne d'Este, the granddaughter of King Louis XII, while his sister Mary married King James V of Scotland. François's brother, Cardinal Charles of Lorraine, was renowned for his learning and lavish style of living.

Foremost among the other houses was that of Montmorency. Anne (in this instance a male name) de Montmorency was for many years the chief minister under Francis I and Henry II. As Constable of France he had charge of the army. His four sons, François, Henri, Charles and Guillaume, became important politically as did his Châtillon nephews: Gaspard de Coligny, Admiral of France, Cardinal Odet (who became a Protestant and fled to England) and François d'Andelot, colonel-general of the infantry.

Only by attending the king's court could nobles hope to benefit from royal gifts of offices or titles. They also shared his authority by serving on his council or by drawing his officials into their clientèles. It was also at court that pressure-groups or factions were formed comprising friends, clients or allies. Nobles advertised their prestige by the magnificence of their dress, the size of their retinues or their proximity to the monarch. Lacking a sufficiently large civil service or standing army, the king needed the support of the great nobles and their clients. By appointing them as provincial governors or lieutenants-general, he tied them to his service. Without their local knowledge he would have had difficulty raising the *compagnies d'ordonnance*.

Clientage was hugely important in sixteenth-century France. The great nobles surrounded themselves with cohorts of dependent nobles and clients. These came from all levels of society and their relationships to the great nobles varied in strength, in permanency and according to the nature of goods and services exchanged. Clientage could be military, domestic or political. A great nobleman commanded a *compagnie d'ordonnance* by virtue of a royal commission, but his troops were tied to him personally: he chose and promoted them. They wore his livery and were forbidden to switch without his consent to another nobleman. The captain's name, reputation and colours were the focus of the company's pride. Clientage could also be domestic. The large household of a great noble offered opportunities of advancement to lesser nobles and others. Aristocratic households were seen as foster homes for aristocratic children, who entered them at the age of 10 or 12. The boys would eventually become pages in a cavalry company, or gain an office at court or an army commission, or they might remain in the household service. Political clientage consisted of local élites –

The Château of Jours-les-Baigneux in Burgundy, built about 1550 by Claude d'Anglure and his wife, Isabeau de Joyeuse. The façade displays a number of gun-ports commanding the approach to the house. (Author's own collection)

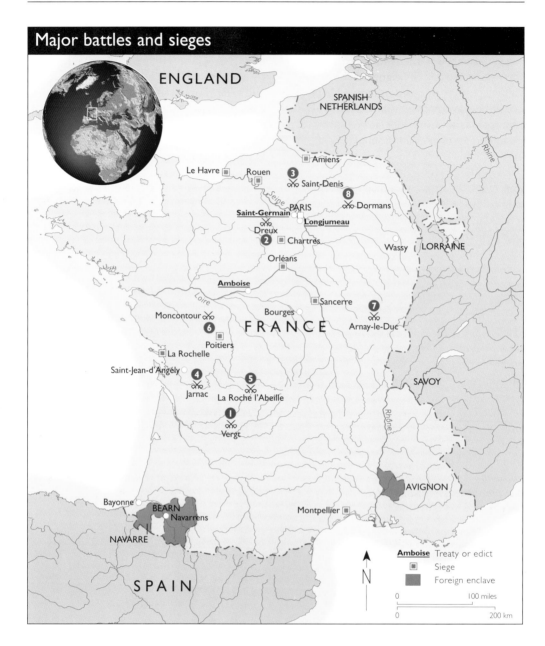

## Major battles and sieges

Several major battles were fought during the early Wars of Religion but the death toll was such that sieges became more important later.

| | |
|---|---|
| 1. 09/10/1562 | 5. 25/06/1569 |
| 2. 19/12/1562 | 6. 03/10/1569 |
| 3. 10/11/1567 | 7. 27/06/1570 |
| 4. 13/03/1569 | 8. 10/10/1575 |

municipal officials, members of parlements, *baillis* and fiscal officials – who owed their offices, titles or pensions to a great nobleman. They would serve him in various ways in return for past favours and in the hope of future patronage. Clientage was evidently dangerous to the king since it might be turned against him. The danger was particularly acute in border provinces, like Champagne, which were vulnerable to foreign attack. Great nobles warned the king not to allow one of their number to rise at the expense of the rest. Their discontent was aroused if one monopolised his favours, leaving less or none for others.

The French nobility did not undergo an overall economic decline in the 16th century as was once believed. That notion rested on false assumptions: that seigneurial rents, fixed by custom and paid in money, were eroded by inflation; and that war, an extravagant life-style and a lack of business sense brought ruin to the nobility. But many rents were paid in kind and were only a part of a seigneur's income, which came mainly from the produce of his domain. Nor was war necessarily ruinous. Only 40 per cent of nobles who served in the army became poorer as a result – 37 per cent grew richer and the rest stayed at about the same level. War could be profitable – much money could be made by capturing a man of rank and demanding a ransom for his release. Finally, the idea that noblemen led extravagant lives needs qualification. Some courtiers did spend lavishly to justify their rank, but they were relatively few. Some families (e.g. the Nevers) did run up debts, but most were surprisingly resilient.

The nobility, like the rest of French society, was affected by the Protestant Reformation. Until the early 16th century France was a uniformly Catholic country, relatively free from heresy. The ideas of the German reformer Martin Luther reached Paris in 1519, but Protestantism was not simply a German import into France. A number of Frenchmen, known as Christian humanists, were already thinking along the same lines as Luther. His doctrine of justification by faith commended itself to them, as did his emphasis on the importance of Scripture. Though Lutheranism was opposed from the start by the theologians of the university of Paris and by the Parlement, King Francis I hesitated before adopting a repressive policy. He had difficulty distinguishing between Christian humanism and Lutheranism. But as time elapsed, French Protestants became more radical. In October 1534 a number of virulent posters attacking the Mass were put up anonymously in Paris and other towns. This was taken as a threat to public order, and brought a violent response from the royal authorities. Many people were arrested and several were burnt at the stake. Among the fugitives from this repression was John Calvin, who eventually settled at Geneva and formulated a Protestant doctrine even further removed from Catholicism than Luther's. Calvin argued that communion was a memorial service, not a sacrifice, as Catholics believed. He viewed the Mass as a blasphemy. In addition to setting out his beliefs in a book, *Institutes of the Christian Religion*, he set up a church in Geneva to which religious exiles from France and elsewhere flocked. He also trained missionaries to carry his ideas abroad. In 1555 they began to infiltrate France. The missionaries were normally sent in response to a request for spiritual guidance from a group of French Calvinists who had set up a church.

The Reformation in France sprang initially from the ranks of the clergy, especially the lower clergy. In time even high-ranking churchmen were also affected. Twelve bishops gave up their sees between 1556 and 1577. During the civil wars, Jean de Saint-Chamond, the former archbishop of Aix, became one of the best commanders of the Protestant army. Around 1560 Calvinism also began to make inroads among the nobility. Clientage helped to spread the new faith, as a noble convert tended to carry his clients with him. In south-west France the process has been compared to the spread of an oil-stain. Many of the 500 people charged with heresy by the Parlement of Toulouse in 1569 were clients of a single Gascon nobleman. A fair proportion of French exiles who went to Geneva were nobles. In the towns, Protestantism began by appealing to the lower orders of society, particularly the artisans, but it is unclear why some groups of workers turned Protestant when others did not. Evidence from Rouen indicates that Protestantism appealed to virtually all social strata and to a wide variety of occupations. Most peasants stood on the sidelines of religious division.

By 1559 French Protestants had achieved a kind of unity. A constitution or 'discipline' drawn up in Poitiers in 1557 regulated the selection of pastors, deacons and elders as well as membership of the churches and the control of morals. Two years later a gathering of representatives from various Protestant churches met in Paris. This meeting, generally regarded as the first national synod, endorsed a 'Confession of Faith'. At this time the majority of Calvinist churches in France were south of the river Loire, in a broad sweep stretching from La Rochelle in the west to the foothills of the Alps in the east. This arc is known as 'the Huguenot crescent' – but Brittany, Picardy, Champagne and Burgundy remained predominantly Catholic. Distance from the centre of government and a strong sense of local independence may have determined this distribution. But French Protestants, who became known as Huguenots, were never more than a minority of the population. Assuming an average of 1,500 communicants per church across the kingdom, we are left with a Protestant population of less than two million; in other words roughly 10 per cent of the total population of some 16 million.

From about 1534 onwards, the French crown committed itself to a policy of religious persecution, involving the censorship of books and the punishment, sometimes by death, of religious dissidents. The last seven years of the reign of Francis I were marked by a sharp rise in the number of prosecutions for heresy. But persecution failed to check the growth of Calvinism. Francis I's successor Henry II denounced Geneva as 'the source of much evil because many heretics are received there and thence disseminate their errors into France'. In 1557 a royal edict mandated the death penalty for heresy, identifying it with sedition. But the Genevan missionaries continued to operate in France. At first they did so as secretly as possible, but sooner or later their activities were bound to come to light. In September 1557 an angry mob broke up a Calvinist meeting in a house in the rue Saint-Jacques in Paris. Noblemen fought their way out of the mêlée, but 132 people were arrested and thrown into prison. In May 1558 a crowd of some 5,000 Huguenots gathered to sing psalms in the Pré-aux-Clercs, a meadow within sight of the royal palace in Paris.

OPPOSITE This fine portrait of Charles IX, King of France (1550–1574), was drawn by Pierre Dumoustier the Elder in 1565. The third son of Henry II and Catherine de' Medici, Charles succeeded his brother, Francis II, on the throne in 1560. As he was still a boy, his mother served as regent until his majority was declared on 17 August 1563. He and Catherine then embarked on a 'grand tour' of France aimed at imposing the peace of Amboise of 1563. In 1567, however, the Huguenots angered him by trying to kidnap him at Meaux and then by blockading him in Paris. Thereafter his attitude towards them may have changed. They blamed him for the Massacre of St. Bartholomew. (Ann Ronan Picture Library)

Henry II ordered such gatherings to stop and prescribed stiffer penalties for heresy. The peace of Cateau-Cambrésis in 1559 enabled him to give more attention to the religious crisis in France. He attended a meeting of the Parlement and was horrified by the religious views expressed by some of its members. He threated to burn one of them, Anne du Bourg, who had dared to criticise his repressive policy.

When the king was accidentally killed soon afterwards, Huguenots hailed the event as an act of God. Henry's successor, Francis II, was only 15. Arguing that he was too young to rule, the Huguenots suggested that the princes of the blood – Antoine de Bourbon, king of Navarre, and his brother, Louis prince de Condé, should be given charge of the government. But before Bourbon could reach the court, François duc de Guise, and his brother, Cardinal Charles of Lorraine, seized control of the government. This ensured that the persecution of Protestants would continue. New laws passed in the autumn of 1559 encouraged popular participation in the repression of heresy. In December 1559 Anne du Bourg was burned at the stake. The Guises, meanwhile, made themselves unpopular by their economic policies. Numerous troops were disbanded without pay. Those who flocked to court to demand redress were threatened with execution. The measures taken by the Guises were doubly offensive because of the exemptions granted to their clients. As a younger branch of the ruling house of Lorraine, they were regarded

as foreign usurpers by Bourbon's followers.
An anonymous pamphlet called on French
nobles to rid the kingdom of foreign tyranny.
Noble discontent and religious dissent
combined to precipitate France into civil war.

In March 1560 a group of lesser Protestant
nobles attempted to gain control of the king
at the château of Amboise in the Loire valley.
The plotters intended no harm to the king,
but hoped to topple his Guise ministers. But
news of the plot leaked out, and the
conspirators were rounded up before they
could act. Some were butchered on the spot,
and their bodies were left hanging from the
château's balconies. Meanwhile, Calvinists
began to worship more openly and to attack
Catholic churches in many parts of France.
A flood of pamphlets denounced the Guises
as usurpers. At an Assembly of Notables in
August 1560, the Chancellor, Michel de
l'Hospital, pressed for a reform of the
Catholic church as a way out of the crisis.
The Huguenots advanced the claims of
Bourbon and Condé against the Guises.
Condé began to raise troops and called on
several great nobles to join him. In December
1560 King Francis II died. He was succeeded
by his brother Charles, who was only 10.

Charles's mother Catherine de' Medici
assumed the regency, and sought to counter
the influence of the Guises by appointing
Bourbon as 'Lieutenant-General of the
Kingdom'. In January 1561 she issued an edict
according to which all religious prisoners were
released and all heresy trials suspended.
Encouraged by her attitude, the Huguenots
redoubled their activities, with the active
encouragement of the pastors in Geneva. One
hundred and fifty missionaries were sent from
Switzerland into France. Calvinists began
systematically to seize Catholic churches and
to destroy statues of the Virgin and saints,
crucifixes and altarpieces.

Excesses like these inevitably triggered a
Catholic backlash. The Paris Parlement
ordered houses used for Protestant

The Tumult of Amboise. In March 1560 an attempt was
made by a group of lesser nobles to gain control of the
court which was residing at the château of Amboise in
the Loire valley. News of the plot leaked out and the
conspirators were rounded up by members of the king's
guard before they could act. This engraving by Jean
Tortorel and Jacques Perrissin shows the king's men,
mounted and armed with pistols, arresting Jean du Barry,
seigneur de La Renaudie, the plot's leader. (Ann Ronan
Picture Library)

## Wars from 1572–1585

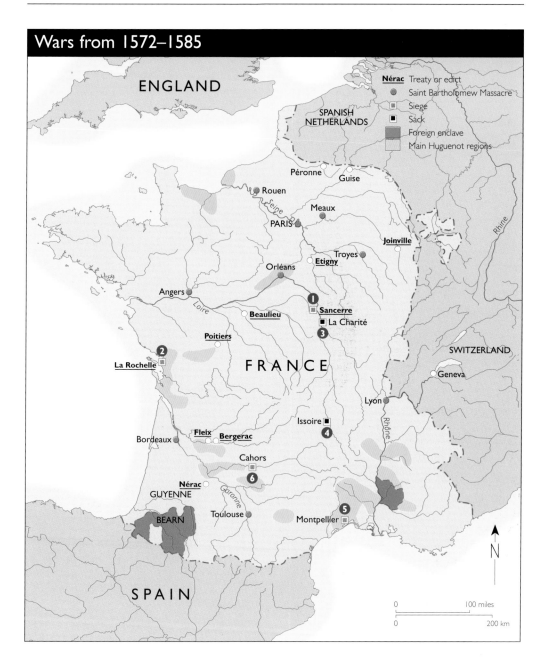

So many Huguenots in northern France were wiped out by the Massacre of St Bartholomew that after 1572 the main area of fighting shifted south of the Loire.

1. 1573
2. 1573
3. 1577
4. 1577
5. 1577
6. 1580

meetings to be razed to the ground. Catholics were urged by preachers and pamphleteers to arm themselves in defence of their faith. In several towns Protestants were massacred. In April 1561 Anne de Montmorency, François duc de Guise and marshal Saint-André formed the Triumvirate, an association for the defence of the Catholic faith. In August 1561 the regent tried to solve the religious crisis by bringing theologians from both sides to a conference at Poissy, but this meeting only revealed the unbridgeable doctrinal gulf between them. In January 1562 the Edict of January allowed

The Tumult of Amboise (March 1560).
This engraving by Tortorel and Perrissin shows the execution of the plotters outside the château of Amboise with members of the court looking on. While La Renaudie's body is swinging from a gibbet, other conspirators are being beheaded or hung from the battlements. Three heads are on a gibbet as a warning to others. (Ann Ronan Picture Library)

OPPOSITE TOP Massacre of Vassy (or Wassy) in Champagne. On 1 March 1562 François duc de Guise was travelling with an armed escort from his home at Joinville to Paris when he came across some Huguenots worshipping in a barn. Following an exchange of insults, the duke's men broke into the barn and a slaughter ensued which helped to trigger the first religious war. (Ann Ronan Picture Library)

OPPOSITE BOTTOM The Château of Vallery in Burgundy. This was acquired in 1548 and rebuilt by Jacques d'Albon, seigneur de Saint-André and a marshal of France, who became one of the so-called Triumvirs in 1561. He was among the Catholics killed at the battle of Dreux in 1562. (Author's own collection)

Huguenots for the first time to worship in public, provided they did so unarmed and outside town walls. On 1 March 1562 the duc de Guise left his home at Joinville for Paris with an armed escort. At Wassy he stumbled across a group of Huguenots worshipping in a barn next to the parish church. A skirmish ensued, and the duke's men burst into the barn, killing a number of worshippers. News of the massacre prompted Catholic rejoicing in Paris, and Guise was given a hero's welcome when he arrived there. Catherine de' Medici tried to pacify the situation by appointing the Cardinal de Bourbon as governor of Paris. He ordered Guise and Condé to leave the capital, but only Condé obeyed. Instead of going to Fontainebleau where the queen mother and the king were staying, Condé left the way clear for his enemies to do so. The Triumvirs went there in force and persuaded Catherine and her son to return with them to Paris. Condé, meanwhile, gathered his supporters at Meaux and made his way south to Orléans, capturing the city on 2 April 1562.

# The crown and the Huguenots

A civil war differs from a foreign war in several ways. A foreign war is usually fought over some disputed territory which can be located precisely on a map. The warring sides – usually two but sometimes more – operate across one or more frontiers thereby producing lines of confrontation or fronts. But a civil war is contained within the borders of a single country and, like a forest fire, it can explode in several places simultaneously. The number of participants is often difficult to determine. There may be more sides than two, and they may call upon military support from outside the country. In 16th-century France the religious wars began as a conflict between two groups of French nobles, one consisting of Catholics loyal to the king and the other of Protestants, who wished to secure religious freedom for themselves and their followers. But as the conflict developed all sorts of new groups and alignments came into being, muddying the waters. In addition to the main belligerents, there were all kinds of noblemen who had the military strength to fight private wars within the larger conflict. This pattern became clearer under King Henry III. Captain Merle, for example, terrorised the hill towns of Gévaudan and Auvergne over 10 years. He would only surrender his conquests in return for compensation and frequently ignored the peace treaties signed by his superiors. Such conduct could easily prompt peasant uprisings. This happened in Provence in 1578 when peasants, called *Razats*, who were made up of both Catholics and Protestants, took up arms mainly in self-defence. Large scale peasant revolts also broke out in Vivarais and Dauphiné. Over the half century or so that the Wars of Religion lasted patterns of motivation changed and new warring sides came into being, prompted by some new political crisis or other.

Thus in 1574 the governor of Languedoc, Henri de Montmorency-Damville, a powerful Catholic nobleman, turned against the government and reached an understanding with the Huguenots. He issued a manifesto complaining of his treatment by the crown, and other noblemen, known collectively as the Malcontents, did likewise. As Henry III tried to negotiate with Damville, the Huguenots in the Midi set up a new military administration, calling itself 'the Union'. Its purpose was not to create a separate state, but to reform the existing one. Supreme authority was vested in a general assembly made up of representatives of the five provinces adhering to the Union. An executive officer, called the Protector, had charge of military affairs. The first was the Prince de Condé, who was succeeded by Montmorency-Damville, and finally by Henri de Navarre. In September 1575 the king's turbulent brother, François d'Alençon, came out in support of the Malcontents and formed a new army at Dreux. Early in October 2,000 German mercenaries invaded Champagne and the threat of a link-up between them and the rebels in the west and south of France prompted Henry III to seek terms. Eventually, a peace was signed which scandalised Catholics by conceding almost complete freedom of worship to the Huguenots. The upshot was the formation of a defensive association, known as the first League, centred on Péronne in Picardy. It soon spread to other French provinces.

In March 1576 the kaleidoscope of allegiances changed again when Montmorency-Damville resumed his allegiance to the king, deserting his Huguenot allies. The death of Henry III's brother, the duc d'Anjou (formerly Alençon) in June 1584 precipitated a new political crisis as it cleared a path to the throne for the Protestant leader,

Henri de Navarre. A new Catholic League headed by Henri, third duc de Guise and his brothers, was set up to exclude him. It allied with Spain and a new warring side came into being as many nobles joined the new movement. Among towns supporting the

An armourer at work. From a sixteenth-century woodcut by Jost Amman. Suits of armour, some of them richly ornamented and costly, were still worn by members of the heavy cavalry or gendarmerie throughout the French Wars of Religion. The best were made in Germany or Italy. (Ann Ronan Picture Library)

League, Paris was the most radical. It turned against Henry III, who was driven to join forces with Henri de Navarre. As they combined their forces to lay siege to Paris, Henry III was assassinated and Navarre succeeded him as King Henry IV, but as long as he remained Protestant he had to fight his way to the throne. So the warring sides changed again, this time with the Catholic League pitted against the crown. Only once Henry IV had become a Catholic was he able slowly to impose his authority on the whole kingdom.

## The Royal Army

In August 1558 King Henry II inspected his army at Pierrepont in Picardy. It consisted of 29,000 infantry and 11,000 cavalry. The occasion was also marked by a great display of firepower. Few European rulers could have put on such a display of military might. Yet the event pointed to some grave weaknesses in the French army. More than 70 per cent of the troops were foreign mercenaries: 8,000 German cavalry and 20,000 Swiss and German infantry. The latter's presence reflected the crown's failure to set up a corps of permanent native infantry. The army was a temporary gathering of units; few of them had got to know each other or train together. The crown lacked the resources to replace losses incurred through fighting, disease or desertion. Nor could it keep the army at full strength in peacetime. When a campaign ended, the army had to be disbanded. Thus, in 1559, Francis II slashed the *gendarmerie* or heavy cavalry from 8,800 men to 6,275. The peacetime army was quite small. Its core was the *gendarmerie* which was organised in companies, called *compagnies d'ordonnance*, each comprising a number of *lances*. A *lance* consisted of a man-at-arms with four horses, two archers with two horses each, and two pages. The number of lances in a company varied in accordance with the social status of its captain. Exceptionally a company would have 100 men, but 40 was the norm. The man-at-arms and his mount wore complete suits of armour, while the archers, who

served as scouts or skirmishers, had only a breastplate and an open helmet. The lance was the main weapon, though portable firearms grew in importance. In the 1550s most companies had 50 mounted arquebusiers attached to them. Captains of companies were always high-ranking noblemen. They were chosen by the king but picked their own subordinates from among their relatives, clients and friends. Although not hereditary by right, a captaincy often passed from father to son, and the men-at-arms and archers were usually lesser nobles.

The gendarmerie was quartered in garrison towns, mainly in frontier provinces. Leave was granted to a quarter of the men at a time by order of seniority and in strict rotation. They were paid out of taxation at musters held every three months, under the supervision of royal commissioners and a treasurer. Until 1548 towns were expected to support the garrisons, but in 1549 a new tax called the *taillon* spread the burden to the whole kingdom. From that time the gendarmerie was expected to pay for its own food and fodder. Normally, the crown maintained between 64 and 69 companies in peacetime or about 2,500 to 2,800 lances representing between 6,275 and 7,100 men. The companies were widely dispersed, albeit unevenly – most were north of the river Loire. When a war broke out, the provincial governors would order captains to gather their men within a fortnight and bring them to a muster where they were counted and paid. Locating them was far from easy and the crown always distrusted the muster rolls.

The army also comprised two kinds of light cavalry though few were maintained in peacetime. The *chevau-légers* were noblemen who had not found a place in the gendarmerie. Although more lightly armoured than the men-at-arms, they were expected to serve as battle cavalry. They were organised in companies of 100 men, forming a regiment under a colonel-general. The *arquebusiers à cheval* were mounted infantry equipped with arquebuses. They rode into action but dismounted to fire their weapons.

Filippo Strozzi (1541–1582) who became one of the principal infantry commanders in the French Wars of Religion. As colonel-general he fought against Coligny at the battle of La Roche L'Abbeille in June 1569 but was taken prisioner. He subsequently took part in naval expeditions against the Spaniards, but was defeated and fatally wounded at the battle of Terceira (July 1582) in the Azores. (Ann Ronan Picture Library)

Arquebuses were still rather primitive weapons. Their rate of fire was slow (about 20 minutes between each shot) and they could not be used in the rain. Arquebusiers served in units of 50 as scouts, escorts and as mobile garrison troops.

By the mid-16th century the main French infantry consisted of 'old' and 'new' bands, each 300 strong. The 'old' bands were based in Picardy and Piedmont and kept on a permanent footing, unlike the 'new' bands, called *aventuriers*, who served only in wartime. Both were recruited mainly from the peasantry. When they were needed, blank commissions were sent out to provincial governors, who distributed them to known captains, who then rounded up the men. The infantry was organised in two commands: one based at Calais, the other at Pinerolo, each under a colonel-general. The first regiments were set up by François, duc de Guise. Each contained 12 companies of 200 men under a camp master (*maître de camp*), a sergeant-major and a camp marshal. From 1547 the infantry as a whole was placed under a single colonel-general, who was always a high-ranking nobleman.

A high proportion of the French infantry in wartime was made up of foreign mercenaries. The Swiss were excellent soldiers – brave, well-disciplined and hardy – but they expected to be paid in full and on time, otherwise they were likely to strike or return to their homeland. Their usefulness on the battlefield was limited by their equipment and organisation. Almost nine out of 10 were armed with pikes, and few wore protective armour. They were commonly relegated to guarding the artillery and trenches. They often refused to storm breaches, though some were prepared to serve as pioneers for extra pay. The French crown also employed German *Landsknechte*. Surviving contracts show how they were raised. A colonel, who received a pension from the crown, contacted a number of captains, who gathered the troops and paid them in advance, usually for three months. The landsknechts were normally assembled in *bandes* or *enseignes* of 300 men. They were valued as shock troops but considered useless in sieges. They were also notorious for their drunkenness and brutality. Not all foreign mercenaries were infantry. From the reign of Henry II onwards, the army also recruited German cavalry armed with flintlock pistols. Known as *Reiter*, they developed a tactic called the *caracole*. They would ride up to the enemy line, discharge their pistols and wheel

This helmet and shield, made for King Charles IX (1550–1574), are now at the Louvre in Paris. They are made of iron, embossed and plated with gold, and are richly decorated with multi-coloured enamels. The helmet was supplied by the goldsmith, Pierre Redon, and the shield by his widow in 1572. The helmet has bas-reliefs depicting ancient scenes of war. The king's monogram - "K"- and oval medallions adorn the shield's border. The central bas-relief depicts the Victory of Marius over Jugurtha, king of Numidia in 107 BC. (Roger-Viollet)

around leaving the way clear for a second wave of reiters to do likewise.

The French artillery was probably the best in Europe. It comprised six types of guns: the cannon, great culverin, *bastarde*, *moyenne*, *faucon*, and *fauconneau*. Only the last four were serviceable in the field, and only the first two for siege work. The organisation of the artillery train was

The cannon made for king Francis I in the early 16th-century bears testimony to the longevity of artillery at the time. After being captured from the French, probably at the battle of Pavia in 1525, it was mounted on a ship, called the *San Juan de Sicilia*, which in 1588 served in the Spanish Armada. She sank in Tobermory Bay (Isle of Mull) where the cannon was salvaged from the wreck about 1740. It is now at Inveraray Castle, Argyllshire. (Author's own collection)

determined by the number and size of the guns. The heavier the gun, the more men and horses were required to man it and the higher the poundage of shot and powder required. A thousand rounds from a cannon used up 32,000 pounds (14,400 kg) of iron shot and 20,000 pounds (9,000 kg) of powder. The artillery was based mainly near the northern border of France and in Paris, where the staff of the Arsenal was headed by the Grand Master of the artillery. He was always a nobleman, as were his subordinate officers, but the skilled workers who serviced the artillery and the gunners were Parisian artisans. When an artillery train was being assembled many other people were recruited for service, including teamsters and pioneers, who were not regarded as part of the army. The teamsters (who transported the guns and munitions) were mostly peasants from the provinces, while the pioneers were the army's riff-raff, poorly paid and much despised. They were formed into work gangs of 200 or less and their duties included mending potholes, digging trenches and mining enemy fortifications. Their tasks were often very dangerous and many deserted.

The commander-in-chief of the army was the king, and in his absence, the Constable of France. This office was held by Anne de Montmorency until 1567. It then remained vacant for 30 years. The king or constable could delegate his authority to the Marshals of France, who were three in number under Henry II. More were appointed later. Their main role was to enforce discipline and they were expected to carry out tours of inspection, each in a third of the kingdom. They were assisted by provosts (*prévôts des maréchaux*) each with a team of subordinates. Anyone other than the king who commanded the army was given the title of lieutenant-general. The camp marshal (*maréchal de camp*) was a senior officer who assigned a place to each man when a camp was being set up. The quartermaster (*maréchal des logis*) saw to the billeting of troops with the assistance of several *fourriers*.

## The Huguenot army

Less is known about the Huguenot army than about the king's because the documentation is scarce. But the two armies were bound to be similar, because the Huguenots had detached themselves from the royal army. Their command structure and numerical strength may have been different, but their fighting methods and weapons were basically the same. As the Huguenots held religious services in the open around 1560, they looked to their nobility for armed protection. Soon each Calvinist church was guarded by a captain and a force of specially-trained men. In November 1560, the Protestant synod of Clairac ordered the churches of Guyenne to begin organising military cadres and, in November 1561, the synod of Sainte-Foy in Upper Guyenne completed the task. Two 'protectors' were appointed, one each for the areas under the jurisdiction of the parlements of Bordeaux and Toulouse.

Colonels were chosen for each colloquy and captains to organise the forces of each church, in preparation for a renewal of persecution. The ministers at Sainte-Foy were ordered to oversee the musters. Eventually, this form of organisation was extended to every French province. The synod of Nîmes in 1562 applied it to that area and other synods followed suit. So by 1562 a military infrastructure was already in place on which the Huguenot 'protector-general', the prince de Condé, could rely when he made his call to arms. The Huguenot forces were funded by gifts from Protestant churches, by property confiscated from Catholics and by tax revenues diverted from royal coffers. The army comprised cavalry and infantry, like that of the king. The infantry companies were 100 to 150 men strong. Only about one-fifth were pikemen; the rest were arquebusiers. By 1562 it seems that some companies were made up entirely of arquebusiers. The nucleus of the heavy cavalry consisted of four companies of the king's army, who went over *en masse* to the Huguenot side – in 1562 François d'Andelot, colonel-general of the king's infantry, defected to the Huguenot side, bringing with him his loyal clientèle. The rest of the army were volunteers raised by the Huguenot leaders among their friends and dependents.

# The first war
# (2 April 1562–12 March 1563)

When he gained control of Orléans on 2 April 1562, Louis prince de Condé asked the ministers and elders of the Calvinist church to send troops for 'the defence of the faith'. According to Claude Haton, a priest of Provins, people from all walks of life, noblemen to artisans, responded to the prince's call. Those who could afford the equipment set off at once as infantry or cavalry, and the rest gave money to the cause. La Noue writes in his *Discours*:

*Noblemen arrived unexpectedly from every side without having been called so that within four days more than five hundred were there… And in this way the most renowned left the provinces with ten, twenty or thirty of their friends carrying arms secretly and lodging in hostelries or paying to camp out until they met the army and the occasion together.*

Six thousand infantry and 2,000 cavalry soon arrived. The nobles provided the heavy cavalry. For infantry, Condé relied heavily on volunteers, mostly from the Midi. They were joined later by 3,000 reiters and 4,000 landsknechts whom François d'Andelot had recruited in the Protestant principalities of Germany. On 8 April, Condé issued a manifesto to the effect that the king and his mother were being held prisoner by the Guises and that, as a prince of the blood, he was duty bound to set them free. The prince also claimed that he was upholding the Edict of January against the men who had shown their wickedness at Wassy. But the Parlement argued that it was for the king, not his subjects, to punish disobedience to the edict. On 19 May Condé compared the Catholic leaders to the Triumvirs of ancient Rome, who had subverted the Roman republic and its laws. Their power, he argued, had been usurped whereas his was 'God-given and natural'.

As well as raising troops at home, Condé looked for assistance from Protestants abroad. While d'Andelot raised 3,000 reiters and 4,000 infantry in Germany, Huguenot agents sought financial and military help in England, but Elizabeth I's main concern was to recover Calais. Under the Treaty of Hampton Court (20 September 1562) her troops occupied Le Havre as a security for the return of Calais. Condé's choice of Orléans as the rallying point for his supporters posed a serious problem for the crown, which had not envisaged using its army against its own subjects. In peacetime, the royal army was distributed among garrison towns along France's northern and north-eastern frontiers. Pulling them back to Paris or another internal position risked exposing the kingdom to foreign invasion and was in itself a difficult operation. Troops on leave at the time had to be found. Once assembled, they had to be equipped, mustered and paid. As French infantry lacked training and expertise, the crown needed to hire foreign mercenaries, which was in itself a lengthy process. The gathering of an artillery train was particularly time-consuming. There was a good store of guns in Paris and elsewhere, but the crown needed hundreds of teamsters with waggons and carts to carry the munitions, and thousands of pioneers. This mobilisation took several weeks and allowed the Huguenots to seize the military initiative. They occupied a number of towns in the Loire valley – Tours, Blois, Angers, Beaugency fell between April and May 1562. Elsewhere, too, they made significant gains. Lyon was taken on 29 April. Some towns fell to Condé as their officials rallied to his cause, while others were seized by armed bands, usually with the help of an urban fifth column. Blaise de Monluc, the king's lieutenant in Guyenne, was bewildered by the speed with which the towns were taken over: 'The Huguenots took us by surprise, so that it is a miracle that this country has survived given the secret intelligence which they had in all the towns.' A chain of command was set up at the same time. Jacques de Crussol became Condé's lieutenant-general in Languedoc, Symphorien de Duras in Guyenne, the baron des Adrets in Dauphiné, and the comte de Tende and Paul de Mouvans in Provence. They raised troops and appointed governors in the more important towns.

The crown, meanwhile, completed its mobilisation. By the end of 1562 it had raised some 288 companies of all types, totalling 48,000 men. About 62 per cent were French and the rest foreign. In July 1562 the main royal army left Paris and marched south. It recaptured Blois and sent out columns under Saint-André and

Silver medal of Antoine de Bourbon, King of Navarre (1518–1562 ). As first prince of the blood, he was urged by the Protestants to assume the French regency following the death of Henry II in 1559, but he moved so slowly that the Guises seized control of the government. Never more than a lukewarm Protestant, he fought for the crown under Charles IX and was fatally wounded at the siege of Rouen in 1562. The reverse of the medal shows Antoine receiving a sceptre from heaven. Facing him are four gods – Jupiter, Aeolus, Neptune, and Time-with their respective attributes. (Osprey Publishing)

Montpensier to regain other towns along the Loire and in Poitou. The army next laid siege to Bourges, capturing it on 31 August. This effectively cut off the Huguenots in Orléans from those in the Midi. The Catholic leaders then decided to march on Rouen, which local Huguenots had taken over. The latter looked to England for help, but it came too late. By the time 200 Scottish soldiers arrived, Rouen was surrounded by 30,000 royal troops. Before a second contingent of 300 English troops turned up, the royalists captured Fort Sainte-Catherine, commanding the south-east approach to the city. Catherine de' Medici pressed for a negotiated settlement, but the Rouennais were divided in their response, and on 21 October the royal forces launched an assault. After five days the city walls were breached. Some Huguenot leaders fled abroad by sea, others slipped away to other towns in Normandy under Protestant control. The royal captains tried to avoid Rouen being sacked by offering their troops a bonus, but despite this the city was sacked for three days. Huguenot houses were looted and even Catholic ones were only spared in return for bribes. Profiteers swooped on the city from as far as Paris to buy cheap booty from the troops. According to the Spanish ambassador, the sack of Rouen cost about 1,000 lives. The most important Catholic

victim was the lieutenant-general, Antoine de Bourbon, king of Navarre, who was succeeded by the cardinal de Bourbon.

Once Rouen had fallen, many royal troops were sent home for the winter, though garrisons were maintained in towns around Orléans. Guise planned to move against the English in Le Havre, but hearing that Condé had left Orléans and was marching on Paris, the duke returned to the capital in haste. He ordered the suburbs to be evacuated, distributed his forces behind the city's walls and refurbished the fortifications. At the same time the government negotiated a truce with Condé. On 10 December the Huguenots broke camp and marched on Chartres, but they were hampered by breakdowns in their artillery train. The troops were also restless, particularly the Germans, who had not been paid. More serious still was the lack of a clear strategy. Chartres being too well defended, the Huguenots looked for another objective. Condé argued for a return to Paris, but Admiral Coligny wanted to march on Normandy, to join forces with the English in

Le Havre. In the end, this plan prevailed. The Huguenots veered towards the north-east, but after crossing the river Eure at Maintenon, they came up against the royal army in the open country south of Dreux. It comprised some 19,000 men, but less cavalry than the Huguenots had.

Early on 19 December the royal army crossed the Eure and formed a line of battle south of Dreux between the villages of Épinay and Blainville. When scouts reported hearing Huguenot drums some two miles to

Siege of Bourges. After the prince of Condé, leader of the Huguenots, had seized Orléans in April 1562 and justified his rebellion in a manifesto, his followers captured a number of important towns, including Rouen and Lyon. Before trying to regain Orléans, the royal army set about isolating the town by capturing others in the vicinity. After recapturing Blois, Tours, Poitiers and Angoulême, it laid siege to Bourges on 19 August. Troops raised in Germany by Andelot arrived too late to save the town but managed to reach Condé. Bourges capitulated on generous terms on 31 August. This effectively cut communications between the Huguenots in Orléans and those in the south of France. Even so, the royal army was unable to capture Orléans and besieged Rouen instead. (Ann Ronan Picture Library)

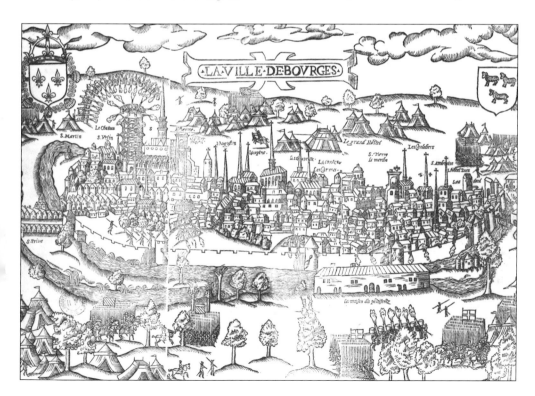

the south, the royal commanders decided to force a battle. Leaving its baggage behind, the royal army moved south, forming a line with the van on the right and the main battle on the left. For some two hours the two armies faced each other.

*Each one*, wrote the Protestant La Noue, *braced himself for battle, contemplating that the men he saw coming were neither Spanish, English, nor Italian, but French, indeed the bravest of them, among whom could be found his own comrades, relatives and friends, and that within the hour it would be necessary to start killing one another.*

Coligny then persuaded Condé to advance. Some Huguenot light cavalry and the reiters fell back as they came under fire from royalist guns whereupon Condé recalled his vanguard. After resuming their battle formation, the Huguenots attacked.

The ensuing battle can be divided into four phases. In the first, which lasted an hour, the Huguenot cavalry charged the left half of the king's army, penetrating the Swiss infantry. Coligny's cavalry routed that of Constable Montmorency, capturing him in the process. Within a short time, the entire left wing of the royal army, except the Swiss, fled with the Huguenots in pursuit. Meanwhile, the right wing of the king's army, under Guise and Saint-André, stood its ground. In the second phase, which lasted another hour, the Swiss bore the brunt of the fighting as they came under attack from Coligny's cavalry. The landsknechts of the Huguenots' second line now joined in the fray only to be thrown back. They barricaded themselves in the village of Blainville. The Swiss then tried to recapture some guns, inviting a new onslaught by the Huguenot cavalry which managed to break up their formation. As the Swiss retreated towards Épinay, the German reiters, shouting 'Victory!', streamed across the plain to Nuisement in order to loot the royal baggage train. Condé and Coligny attempted to rally their cavalry which was now dispersed all over the plain. The Huguenot infantry, in

the meantime, had lost its cavalry support. In the third phase of the battle, Guise and Saint-André launched an attack which seemed to sweep the Huguenots from the field. A unit of gendarmes, backed by Spaniards, wreaked havoc among the Huguenot infantry. Condé was captured as the Huguenot cavalry retreated, tired and disorganised, through woods on the east side of the field. The royalists seemed assured of victory and Guise approached Blainville to secure the surrender of the landsknechts. However, the battle now entered its last phase, as Coligny emerged from the woods with about 1,000 horse. With more cavalry than the enemy, the Huguenots seemed set to win, but they came under withering fire from Guise's arquebusiers. As darkness fell, it became difficult to tell friend from foe. Coligny sounded the retreat and the Huguenot cavalry withdrew from the field which was now strewn with corpses.

The bitterly cold night which followed must have taken its toll of the wounded. Casualties among the Swiss were especially heavy. Ambroise Paré, the famous surgeon, reported: 'I observed for a good league all around the ground completely covered. The estimate was twenty five thousand dead or more, all dispatched in less than two hours.' Paré treated many noblemen and poor soldiers, including many Swiss captains. For some time there was uncertainty as to who had won the battle of Dreux. Although early reports suggested a Huguenot victory, it soon became clear that the crown had won – but the price had been heavy. Dreux was one of the bloodiest battles of the century. Paré's estimate may be an exaggeration. One modern estimate puts the number of dead at 6,000. Both sides suffered badly. The Huguenots admitted 3,000 casualties, not counting 1,500 landsknechts who had surrendered to Guise. The French infantry were particularly hard hit. 'We pursued them', wrote a Spaniard, 'and inflicted great carnage, killing them like sheep.' Another wrote 'without losing more than six men, we broke them and killed 3,000 of them'. Casualties on the royalist side may have been heavier still. Probably more than 1,000 Swiss died, including their colonel and most of their officers. All but one of the cavalry commanders were killed, wounded or captured. Saint-André was murdered after he had been taken prisoner. The total of casualties on both sides may have been around 10,000.

After this defeat, the Huguenot army withdrew to Orléans. Enough infantry had survived to garrison the city while Coligny reorganised the cavalry. The royal army, too, badly needed to recuperate. If some of its units had survived almost unscathed, others – notably the Swiss – had been all but wiped out. The cavalry was so crippled that Guise had to create 17 new companies. Funds, too, were urgently required. The political scene was transformed as a result of the battle. Guise, who was appointed lieutenant-general after Montmorency's capture, was the only member of the Triumvirate to survive. Both Montmorency and Condé were prisoners. As La Noue writes in his memoirs, the battle was unusual in that the commanders on both sides were taken prisoner. The new situation allowed Catherine de' Medici to negotiate peace. She listened to overtures from Condé, who pressed for a national council to meet within six months, but Admiral Coligny (who had replaced Condé as the Protestant commander) wanted to continue the fight. In January 1563 he left d'Andelot in charge of Orléans and went to Normandy where he recovered a few towns. On 3 February 1563 Guise laid siege to Orléans. Thirteen days later he was assassinated as he was about to launch an assault. The assassin was a Huguenot

The Battle of Dreux (19 December 1562). This was the first serious engagement of the religious wars and an extremely bloody one. After Rouen had capitulated to the royal army on 26 October 1562, the Huguenots tried to link up with an English expeditionary force which had occupied Le Havre. After crossing the river Eure at Maintenon, they encountered the royal army in open country south of Dreux. For some two hours the two armies faced each other. The Huguenots were the first to attack. The Constable Montmorency was soon taken prisoner. Later, it was the turn of the Huguenot leader, Condé, to be captured. Another casualty was marshal Saint-André who was murdered after falling into Huguenot hands. The number of casualties proved so heavy on both sides that they tried thereafter to avoid pitched battles. (Ann Ronan Picture Library)

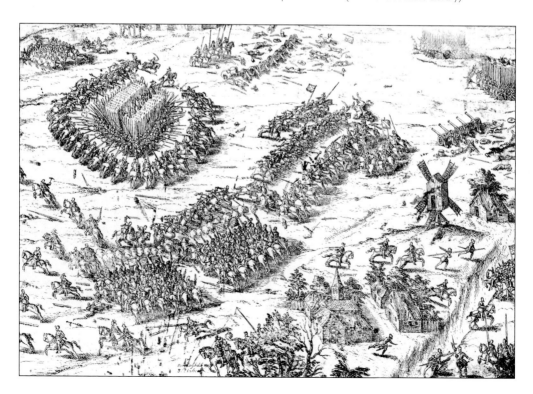

## Battle of Dreux, 19 December 1562

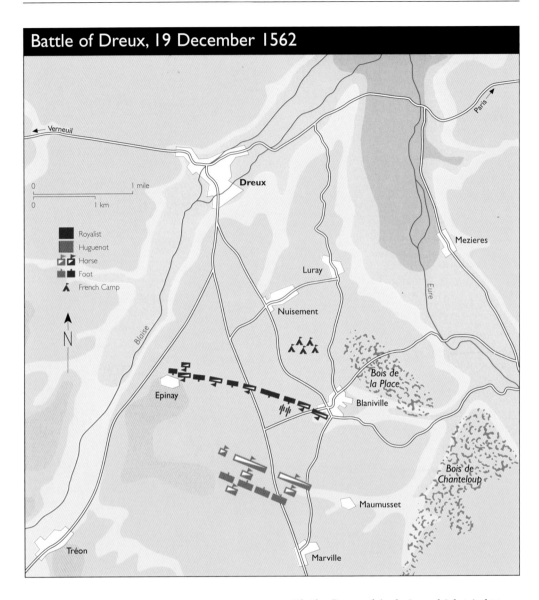

The first major battle of the religious wars was fought near Dreux on 19 December 1562. The Huguenots were defeated, but both sides suffered heavy casualties.

nobleman, called Poltrot de Méré. The duke's widow and other members of his family accused Coligny of instigating the murder. He denied the charge, but made no secret of his satisfaction over the duke's death. Henceforth, a new element entered the civil war in the form of a vendetta between the houses of Guise and Châtillon, which the crown vainly attempted to assuage. On 12 March 1563 the first religious war ended

with the Peace of Amboise, which tried to remove the causes of conflict by imposing a compromise. While allowing freedom of conscience for everyone, it restricted Protestant worship. Noblemen were allowed to worship on their estates or in their homes according to their judicial status, but other Protestants could only do so in the suburbs of one town per *bailliage*, or in towns where they had done so on 7 March 1563. Protestant worship was banned in and around Paris. At the same time, all church property was to be restored and all prisoners of war and religious prisoners set free. Condé

was discharged of any obligation for royal revenues he had seized; he was also pardoned for minting money, manufacturing guns and munitions and fortifying towns. All associations were banned, as were fund-raising, the raising of troops and armed gatherings.

The compromise peace pleased no one. Protestants mourned the Edict of January, which had allowed them to worship anywhere outside walled towns. Mobs in Orléans destroyed churches they were meant to return to the Catholic authorities. Catholic opposition to the peace was even more virulent. In Rouen, the parlement refused for a time to register the edict of pacification, and banned any Huguenot who had shared in the seizure of the city from returning to it. Yet the peace lasted four years and enabled both sides in the civil war to combine in an effort to drive the English out of France. A large army under the command of Marshal Brissac and the Constable Montmorency, laid siege to Le

The assassination of François second duc de Guise, outside Orléans. On 5 February 1563 Guise laid siege to Orléans. Thirteen days later, as he was planning an assault, a Huguenot nobleman, called Poltrot de Méré, shot him in the back. The death of the duke who had become a national hero caused outrage among French Catholics. His widow, Anne d'Este, and her children accused the Huguenot leader, Admiral Coligny, of having instigated the murder. They plotted revenge which they were eventually able to achieve in August 1572 during the Massacre of St. Bartholomew, when Coligny was murdered by a group of armed men led by Guise's son, Henri. (Ann Ronan Picture Library)

Havre in July. The English commander, the earl of Warwick, had not fortified the town, which was also stricken by plague. On 27 July, after a bombardment lasting three days the town surrendered. Soon afterwards, the young King Charles IX visited Rouen with his mother and the rest of the court, and it was here, on 17 August, that his majority was proclaimed. In March 1564 the king and his mother embarked on an extensive progress across the kingdom. Its

ABOVE The Peace of Amboise (12 March 1563). The first war of religion ended with a peace treaty negotiated by Condé and Montmorency who had both been captured at Dreux. They met on an island in the Loire river watched by the queen-mother, Catherine de'Medici, and royal councillors. The Huguenots were seriously divided about the terms. While Condé was prepared to make concessions for the sake of the peace, the Huguenot pastors whom he consulted proved far less compliant. In the end a treaty was signed on 12 March which was confirmed by the Edict of Amboise on 19 March. It was badly received by both sides. Coligny declared that it had inflicted more damage on the Protestant cause than its enemies had done over 10 years. (Ann Ronan Picture Library)

OPPOSITE The three Châtillon brothers: from left to right, Odet de Chatillon (1517-1571) who turned Protestant after being a cardinal and died in England as a religious exile; Gaspard de Coligny (1519-1572), who was Admiral of France, commanded the Huguenot forces after the death of Condé in 1569 and was murdered in the Massacre of St Bartholomew, and François seigneur d'Andelot (1521-1569), who was an important Huguenot captian in the first two wars. The three brothers were the nephews of the Constable, Anne de Montmorency, who, for his part, championed the Catholic cause. This engraving, after a drawing by Marc du Val, dates from around 1579. (Roger-Viollet)

purpose was twofold: to present the king to his people, but also to curb the independence of the provincial parlements and municipal authorities. Charles IX intervened in the affairs of almost every town on his progress and wherever possible tried to strike a fair balance between the religious parties. By 1 May 1566, when the court returned to Paris, France seemed more or less at peace.

# From the 'Surprise de Meaux' to the siege of Rouen

## The second war (1567–68)

In 1566 a serious Calvinist uprising broke out in the Spanish Netherlands. Fearing a repetition in his own dominions of the troubles in France, Philip II of Spain ordered the duke of Alba to crush the revolt. Starting out from Milan, he led an army north along the so-called 'Spanish Road' which skirted the eastern border of France. No one in France, not even the government, knew his intended destination. The possibility that Alba would invade France in support of the Guises and the Catholic cause could not be ruled out. As a defensive measure King Charles IX hired 6,000 Swiss mercenaries. Ostensibly their purpose was to guard the French frontier, but the Huguenots feared that they might be used against themselves and decided on a pre-emptive strike. They

planned to take control of the royal court while it was at Montceaux. But the success of the operation depended on secrecy and Catherine de' Medici soon got wind of the Huguenot mobilisation. On 24 September Charles IX ordered the Swiss, who were at Château-Thierry, to join him in haste. He and his mother then took refuge behind the walls of Meaux before returning to Paris, but near Lagny the royal party found its path blocked by the Huguenots. While fruitless negotiations took place, the king and his mother reached Paris. Catherine described

Tapestry, now at the château of Ecouen, which reproduces in reverse an engraving of 1570 by Perrissin and Tortorel. It depicts the battle of Saint-Denis (10 November 1567) between the Huguenots and Louis, prince de Condé, and a royal army under the 74-year-old Constable of France, Anne de Montmorency, who was fatally wounded in the battle. (Roger-Viollet)

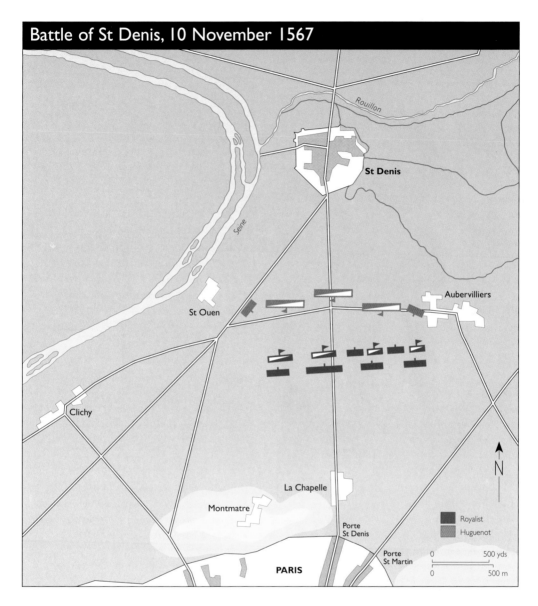

## Battle of St Denis, 10 November 1567

On 10 November 1567 the royal army under the Constable Montmorency successfully attacked a smaller Huguenot force which was blockading Paris, but the Constable was fatally wounded.

the Huguenot action, known as the *Surprise de Meaux*, as 'the greatest wickedness in the world' while Charles IX vowed to hunt down the Huguenots into their homes and beds. They now added insult to injury by blockading the capital. After pitching camp at Saint-Denis, they set fire to windmills near Paris's northern gate. The Parisians hastened to arm themselves, and Montmorency summoned infantry from Picardy and Lyon. Meanwhile several towns including Orléans and La Rochelle declared for the Huguenots. As both sides prepared for war, Condé

repeated demands made in 1562, including the expulsion of all foreigners from the king's council, the exclusion from power of the queen-mother and the calling of the Estates-General. On 7 October the Huguenot leaders were ordered to appear before the king or to admit that they were rebels.

The two sides were numerically unequal. While the Huguenots had 4,000 infantry and

Anne de Montmorency (1493-1567) Constable of France and governor of Languedoc. One of the wealthiest noblemen in France with lands in 17 provinces and seven châteaux, including Chantilly and Ecouen, he served Francis I and Henry II as a minister and military commander, before losing power to the Guises under Francis II. In 1561 he formed an alliance in defence of the Catholic faith, nicknamed the Triumvirate, with François de Guise and marshal Saint-André. Captured at the battle of Dreux, he was released as a result of the peace of Amboise. In 1567, at the age of 74, he led the royal forces to victory at the battle of Saint-Denis, but was fatally wounded and died two days later. (AKG, Berlin)

2,000 cavalry, the royal army comprised 16,000 infantry, 3,000 cavalry and 18 cannon. On 10 November Montmorency launched an attack on the Huguenots who were stretched out in a single line between the villages of Saint-Ouen and Aubervilliers. The battle of Saint-Denis began with a bombardment by the royal guns, but Montmorency ordered his men to attack before its effect could be assessed or his infantry deployed. As the left wing of the royal army advanced, Coligny threw back the inexperienced Parisian volunteers. Condé then charged, breaking through the centre of the royal line with ease. In the ensuing mêlée, the old Constable was fatally wounded. His place as commander of the royal army was filled by the king's brother, Henri duc d'Anjou. Despite his success, Condé had not enough troops to continue blockading Paris. Abandoning his camp, he

dashed eastwards hoping to join forces with a German army led by John Casimir, son of the Elector Palatine, which was on its way to help him. The king's army (the largest ever put in the field during the civil wars) set off in pursuit. It consisted of almost 38,000 troops, two-thirds infantry and one-quarter cavalry. The rest were labourers, artillerymen and camp-followers. The army caught up with Condé on 22 November near Châlons-sur-Marne, but the Huguenots managed to slip away under cover of night. On 11 January 1568 they joined John Casimir's army at Pont-à-Mousson. Giving up the chase, Anjou set up camp at Vitry-le-François where he was joined by forces commanded by Aumale and Nevers. The royal army was now almost 60,000 strong, yet its commanders were reluctant to fight. Mindful of the losses suffered by the gendarmerie at Saint-Denis, they engaged in delaying tactics, hoping that the onset of winter and lack of funds would cause the enemy to melt away. On 23 March 1568 the Peace of Longjumeau was signed. This restored the Edict of Amboise without the additions restricting Protestant worship. Huguenots were promised a complete amnesty and in secret clauses, the king undertook to help pay the wages of John Casimir's reiters. They were soon disbanded and returned home, leaving behind them a trail of destruction. Though seemingly generous to the Huguenots, the peace may have been simply a trap. For the Catholics remained under arms after the Huguenots had disbanded.

by the time it reached Montpellier. On 3 January 1570 Coligny joined forces with Gabriel de Lorges, comte de Montgomery, who had been fighting a successful campaign in Béarn. A serious quarrel between the royal governors, Blaise de Monluc and Henri de Montmorency-Damville, offered the Huguenots an almost clear run in Upper Guyenne and Languedoc. Growing rich on the spoils of war, they besieged Toulouse from 22 January to 20 February 1570. A chain of fortresses reaching far inland from the Atlantic coast gave them control of the Loire valley. Provence and Lower Languedoc were theirs too, while Montauban, Albi and Castres formed a line of defence in the west. The Huguenots were less strong in Upper Languedoc, yet held a number of towns. They had a chain of fortified strongholds stretching north from Béarn to Bergerac and Angoulême. Coligny originally intended to winter in Gascony and Guyenne. He hoped to bring up heavy artillery from Béarn and to take all the towns on the Garonne, even to blockade Bordeaux. But he soon came to realise that the crown would not make peace as long as fighting was confined to south-west France, so he decided to bring the war nearer to Paris. After besieging Toulouse

unsuccessfully, he marched on Carcassonne, then up the Rhône valley to Chalon-sur-Saône. The crown watched helplessly as provincial governors failed to stop Coligny's advance. Montmorency-Damville, the governor of Languedoc, seemed reluctant to pursue him. Two other marshals, François de Montmorency and François de Vieilleville, were equally lethargic. Their attitude reflected divisions among the nobility. Even the king's councillors were divided over the conduct of the war. As Coligny approached Paris, moderate voices grew louder.

Battle of Moncontour (3 October 1569). After failing to capture Poitiers, the Huguenot leader, Coligny, tried to march to the relief of La Charité-sur-Loire but was intercepted by a numerically superior royal army commanded by the duc d'Anjou outside Moncontour. Anjou disposed of 9,000 horse, 15,000 foot, 6,000 Swiss and 15 guns, Coligny of only 6,000 horse, 8,000 arquebusiers, 4,000 landsknechts, six cannon and two culverins. In the ensuing battle, the Swiss pikemen, protected by their arquebusiers and forming an 'iron hedgehog', threw back the Huguenot cavalry, which retired abandoning its artillery. A dreadful slaughter ensued as the Swiss killed 4,000 Germans and 1,500 French. Though urged to pursue the enemy, Anjou allowed Coligny to retire to Montauban and, in the spring of 1570, to shut himself up in La Charité. (Ann Ronan Picture Library)

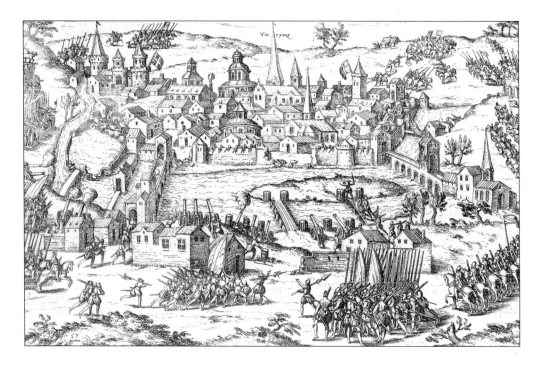

Siege of Poitiers (1569). In the summer of 1569 the Huguenot leader, Coligny, wanted to capture Saumur as the first step towards carrying the war to the Paris region, but his German troops, keen as always on sack and loot, persuaded him to besiege Poiters instead. The operation began on 24 July. The defenders, led by the comte de Lude, disposed of heavy artillery newly arrived from Paris and of a few hundred cavalry under the young Henri, third duc de Guise. They flooded the meadows outside the town by altering the course of the river Clain. A diversionary attack by Anjou on Châtelleraut gave Coligny a pretext for lifting the siege on 7 September. (Ann Ronan Picture Library)

Nevertheless, the crown tried to make a stand on the Loire. An army under Marshal Cossé engaged Coligny at Arnay-le-Duc in Burgundy on 27 June, but failed to check his advance. Picking up guns and reinforcements at Sancerre and La Charité, Coligny drew closer still to the capital, knowing that the king now wanted peace. But Coligny did not want to repeat the Longjumeau experience – this time he looked for solid guarantees.

The upshot was the Peace of Saint-Germain, signed in August 1570, which for the Huguenots marked a major advance on earlier settlements. They were now given four security towns (La Rochelle, Montauban, La Charité and Cognac) for two years. In addition they were allowed limited rights of worship, except in Paris and at court.

## The fourth war (1572–1576)

Catherine de' Medici took advantage of the peace to arrange a marriage between her daughter, Marguerite, and the young Huguenot leader, Henri de Navarre. Her plan may have been to heal the religious division of the nation. If so, it proved a disastrous failure, for the marriage was highly unpopular among both Catholics and Protestants. Paris was a fanatically Catholic city where violence against Huguenots was a daily event. It was asking for trouble to bring Catholic and Protestant nobles together in Paris for the wedding, which took place at Notre-Dame on 18 August 1572 and was followed by four days of glittering festivities. But on 22 August, Coligny was shot as he was walking back to his residence from the Louvre. He was only slightly wounded, but the attempt on his life prompted a wave of violence in the capital. As the Huguenots called for the assailant to

# Coligny's march and foreign military aid

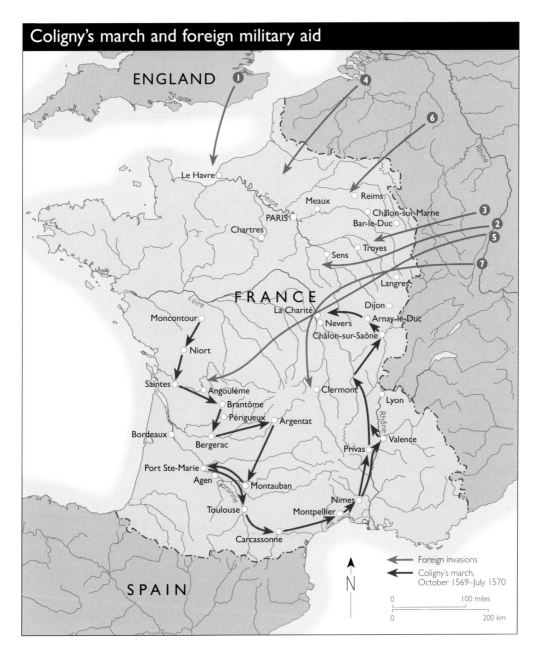

ENGLAND

Le Havre

Meaux    Reims
PARIS    Châlon-sur-Marne
Chartres    Bar-le-Duc

Sens    Troyes

Langres

FRANCE
La Charité    Dijon
Moncontour    Nevers    Arnay-le-Duc
Châlon-sur-Saône

Niort

Saintes    Angoulême    Clermont
Brantôme    Lyon
Périgueux    Argentat
Bordeaux    Valence
Bergerac    Privas
Port Ste-Marie
Agen    Montauban
Toulouse    Nîmes
Montpellier
Carcassonne

SPAIN    N

⟵  Foreign invasions
⟵  Coligny's march,
October 1569–July 1570

0    100 miles
0    200 km

be punished, Catholics feared an uprising. On 23 August the king and his council decided that 'it was better to win a battle in Paris, where all the leaders were, than to risk it in the field and fall into a dangerous and uncertain war'. Early on 24 August a group of armed men led by Guise went to Coligny's house and murdered him in cold blood, thereby avenging the murder in 1563 of Guise's father. Soon afterwards, the tocsin of

Following the Huguenot defeat at Moncontour , Admiral Coligny decided to force the crown to make peace by threatening Paris. He staged a spectacular march across Languedoc and up the Rhone valley. During the wars the Huguenots received military assistance from England, the Netherlands and Germany.

1. Warwick, 1562
2. Andelot, 1562
3. Casimir, 1567
4. Orange, 1568
5. Zweibrücken, 1569
6. Thore, 1575
7. Casimir-Condé, 1576

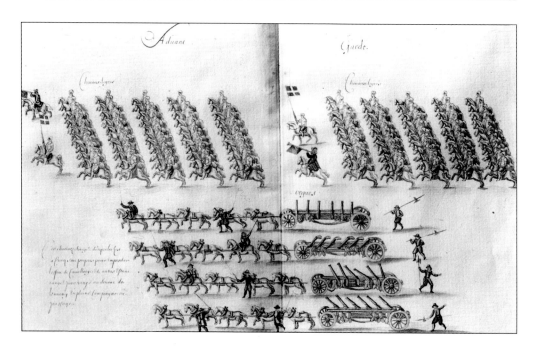

This illustration from a 16th-century manuscript by Vasselieu (1574) shows the vanguard of an army. Light cavalry (*chevau-légers*) are escorting carts pulled by horses and laden with arquebuses. More lightly armoured than men-at-arms, the *chevau-légers* were organised in companies of 100 men each, forming a regiment under a colonel-general. (Roger-Viollet)

the church of Saint-Germain l'Auxerrois gave the signal for one of the bloodiest massacres in European history. Over several days, thousands of Huguenots were butchered in Paris and other towns sometimes with the encouragement of the royal authorities. Such an event inevitably had a powerful effect on the course of the wars. For one thing, it seriously weakened the Protestant cause. Many Huguenots saved themselves by abjuring their faith. At least 3,000 in Rouen alone are known to have turned Catholic. Others preferred to emigrate, mainly to England. Yet the Huguenot movement survived in the west and south, where it controlled a number of fortified towns. The massacre also had the effect of poisoning relations between the Huguenots and the crown, for the king admitted responsibility for the murder of their leaders. The Huguenots could no longer claim, as they had done in the past, that they were fighting

the king's evil advisers, not the king himself. Even so, they did not turn republican. They remained monarchists at heart, while hoping that one day their own leader, Henri de Navarre, would become king. At present, however, he was a prisoner at the French court, having been forced to give up his faith.

Charles IX still hoped that the peace would hold, but his attempts to gain control of La Rochelle by peaceful means were strongly resisted. The inhabitants rejected his choice of governor, and it soon became clear that the town would have to be taken by force. Anjou was put in charge of the operation, but mobilising for the siege of La Rochelle proved difficult. Almost every part of the kingdom was made to contribute in some way. A huge effort went into marshalling the artillery. This comprised 42 cannon and great culverins, 354 personnel from the Paris Arsenal, 220 teamsters and 4,850 pioneers. Transporting such a train from Paris to La Rochelle, mostly overland, proved arduous. Supplying the army with food and drink was also complicated. The merchants of Niort promised to supply 30,000 loaves, 10,800 pints of wine and 20,000 lbs of beef each day. In January 1573 the cost of preparing the siege amounted to 534,000 *livres* of which only 287,000 had so far been paid. Pending Anjou's arrival, Marshal Biron set about blockading La Rochelle, but his efforts were hampered by bad weather, mutiny among his troops and by sorties by the Rochelais. By 11 February, when Anjou arrived with 25,000 troops, La Rochelle was encircled, but approach trenches still had to be dug. The harbour had been only partially blocked by the sinking of ships. The shore batteries were also incomplete. Anjou completed the harbour's closure. By 20 April trenches leading to the *bastion de l'Évangile* were ready. Between February and June, Anjou launched eight major assaults. The first, on 7 April, was preceded by a furious bombardment which breached the town's wall. About 200 nobles wearing cuirasses and carrying small shields were ordered to scale the breach, but many were roasted alive as they came under a hail of incendiary devices. The assault merely gained a toe-hold at the foot of the bastion. Anjou wanted to renew the assault next day, but finding that he had only 100 cannon

balls left, he had to get some more from the royal fleet offshore. On 8 April the defenders laid down a smokescreen so thick that it seemed like 'a pit of Hell'. On 10 April another royal assault was thrown back. Anjou complained that so many of his men were deserting that he expected in the end to find himself alone. Work on the approaches came to a virtual standstill as only 400 pioneers remained. On 14 April a mine exploded, bringing down part of the bastion, but also throwing up tons of rock and earth on to Anjou's troops, causing numerous casualties. Supplies in his camp

Siege of La Rochelle (1572–1573). Under the peace of Saint-Germain (August 1570) the Huguenots were given La Rochelle as a security town for two years. In October 1572 the inhabitants refused to admit the governor appointed by the crown and called on English aid. A royal army commanded by the king's brother, Henri duc d'Anjou, and marshal Biron, besieged the town as from November. On the landward side La Rochelle was protected by a dry moat and walls reinforced at intervals by bastions, the most famous being the bastion de l'Évangile. Several assaults were launched only to be repelled with heavy royal losses. Anjou's election as king of Poland gave him a face-saving pretext to lift the siege on 24 June 1573. (Ann Ronan Picture Library)

also began to run out. Gendarmes who could no longer feed their horses were sent home. The royal infantry was below half strength, and lack of gunpowder reduced the artillery to virtual silence.

On 23 May Anjou received 6,000 Swiss reinforcements, but they were virtually useless, being armed only with pikes. Taking advantage of the confusion that attended their coming, the Rochelais effected a sortie. They spiked four royal guns and captured a number of standards. On 30 May Anjou blamed the cowardice of his troops for the failure of another assault. 'After seeing what I saw that

day', he wrote to the king, 'I am almost ashamed to be French'. He disbanded 60 companies of infantry. After two more unsuccessful assaults, he complained to the king of insufficient artillery, manpower and food. Meanwhile, Anjou learnt that he had been elected king of Poland. This gave him an excuse to end the siege honourably. A truce was soon arranged; then peace. Anjou's camp was broken up, and the duke returned to Paris. Royal losses during the siege were out of all proportion to the results obtained. The army suffered at least 6,000 battle casualties and probably as many again caused by sickness

The Massacre of St Bartholomew's Day (24 August 1572). This painting, now in Lausanne, is by François Dubois, a Huguenot who settled in Switzerland. Though he seems not to have witnessed the massacre in Paris, his painting is a graphic illustration of its horrors. The body of Admiral Coligny is being thrown out of a window of his residence while one of his friends is fleeing over the roof tops. Catherine de' Medici stands outside the gateway to the Louvre looking down at the bodies of some of the victims. (AKG, Berlin)

large-scale military operations. A year was about as long as he could afford to fight – hence the brevity of the later civil wars. Soon after the massacre of St Bartholomew, Charles IX appointed Montmorency-Damville, governor of Languedoc, as lieutenant-general in the Lyonnais, Dauphiné and Provence. He was expected to ensure the security of towns loyal to the king and to reconquer the rebellious ones. In February 1573 Damville systematically besieged the latter, his ultimate objective being Nîmes, the main Huguenot stronghold in Languedoc. Charles IX ordered him to enforce the recent peace, but failed to give him enough money or troops. While talks continued, a truce was declared in the south, but the Huguenots used it to consolidate their position.

In February 1574 a Huguenot plot to free the princes of Condé and Navarre coincided with a Huguenot uprising in Lower Normandy, Poitou and the Rhône valley. Although desperately poor, Charles IX issued a call to arms. Three armies were assembled: one in Normandy under Matignon, another in Poitou under Montpensier and the third in Dauphiné under Henri de Bourbon. They recaptured towns which had fallen to the Huguenots, including Domfront, Saint-Lô, and Carentan in Normandy as well as Fontenay and Lusignan in Poitou. In April 1574 another plot was discovered at court. The plan this time was for Alençon and Navarre to escape from the court to Sedan where Turenne was to join them with 300 horse. The two princes were put under house arrest, and marshals Montmorency and Cossé were imprisoned. Soon afterwards, on 30 May, Charles IX died. His mother, Catherine de' Medici, declared herself regent pending the return from Poland of her son, Henri, who now became King Henry III. On 18 June she relieved

and desertion. The casualty rate was especially high among the officers. Two hundred and sixty-six were killed according to an official list. Even allowing for France's rising population, it would have been difficult for the crown to make up such losses with adequately trained officers. Likewise, the siege emptied the kingdom of guns and munitions faster than they could be replenished. The royal treasury was also seriously depleted. Its gross revenue amounted to 14.8 million *livres* per annum in theory, but only 4.5 million was available in practice. From the mid-1570s onwards the king could no longer afford

Montmorency-Damville of his command in the Midi, driving him into the arms of the Huguenots who were organising a federal state there. In July 1574 Henri, prince de Condé, was appointed as its 'governor-general and protector' and Damville as governor and lieutenant-general in Languedoc. Following his return to France in September, Henry III tried to detach Damville from his Huguenot allies but the governor's reply was a manifesto in which the king's foreign councillors were blamed for all France's ills. This was only one of several declarations by noblemen, known collectively as the 'Malcontents', who constituted a new force, more political than religious. Following the massacre of St Bartholomew, many Catholic nobles came to believe that the religious conflict was playing into the hands of sinister forces in the government who aimed to destroy France's ancient liberties. The Malcontents resented royal favouritism in the distribution of gifts and honours.

# The fifth war (November 1574 – May 1576)

In January 1575 Henry III left Avignon for northern France, and on 13 February he was crowned at Reims. In the west, Montpensier captured a number of small towns commanding the approaches to La Rochelle for the king. As the war seemed to be getting nowhere, Henry III tried to negotiate. On 11 April he received a deputation from Damville, who made sweeping demands. Meanwhile, fighting continued in many parts of France, but the pattern of conflict had changed. Instead of large armies, forces of a few thousand men, each under a captain,

OPPOSITE François, duc de Montmorency (1530–1579), eldest son of the Constable, Anne de Montmorency. In 1556 he became governor of Paris and the Ile-de-France and in 1560 a marshal of France. Although a firm Catholic, he upset the Parisians by his willingness to compromise with the Huguenots. In 1574 he was accused of complicity in a plot at court and imprisoned along with his cousin, marshal Artus de Cossé. He died in 1579. (Roger-Viollet)

carried out raids against towns and villages, sprang ambushes and generally caused mayhem in the countryside. Pillage, rape and the extortion of ransoms were the order of the day. Religion seemed less important now than settling old scores or satisfying private ambition or lust. On 13 September the king's brother, François d'Alençon, fled from the court in Paris to Dreux, where he issued a manifesto repeating Damville's earlier demands. His defection gave the Malcontents legitimacy by association with a prince of the blood. Their movement grew in strength as 1,000 nobles rallied to Alençon's standard. Early in October, an army of 2,000 German reiters under John Casimir invaded Champagne in support of the Huguenots. The alarming prospect of a link-up between them and the rebels in the south and west of France prompted Henry III to send his mother on a peace errand. She met Alençon at Chambord in late September. He asked for the release of the two marshals which Henry III reluctantly conceded. Under a truce, signed at Champigny on 21 November, Alençon was promised five towns as security, while Condé was promised Mézières. The reiters were to receive 500,000 *livres* on condition they stayed east of the Rhine.

Catherine hoped that the truce would lead to peace, but the governors of Angoulême and Bourges refused to hand over their cities to Alençon. Nor could the advance of the reiters be halted. Although some were defeated by Guise at Dormans on 10 October, more than 25,000 crossed the Meuse on 9 January 1576. While the defences of Paris were strengthened, part of the royal army gathered at Gien under the king's command. The rest, under Guise's brother, the duc de Mayenne, stood by at Vitry-le-François. But the royal troops, unpaid and in rags, could only shadow John Casimir's army as it pushed south, reaching Dijon on 31 January and Moulins on 4 March. To make matters worse the truce of Champigny proved ineffective. Most of the towns that had been promised to Alençon refused to admit his men. In December 1575 he accused the chancellor, Birague, of trying to poison him and made this an excuse for breaking the

John Casimir's army on the move. During the second
religious war the Huguenots turned to the German
Protestant princes for armed assistance. Only Frederick
III duke of Bavaria responded positively. He sent them
money and an army under his son, John Casimir
(1543–1592) which consisted of 6,500 reiters and
3,000 landsknechts. They met up with Condé and
Coligny outside Châlons on 16 January 1568, but when
the Huguenots failed to pay their wages, the German
troops ransacked the countryside. Under the peace of
Longjumeau (March 1568) the king agreed to pay them
on condition that they rapidly evacuated the kingdom.
(Ann Ronan Picture Library)

truce. He was joined by Turenne with
3,000 arquebusiers and 400 horse.

Henry III's predicament grew worse by the
day. In Normandy there was a Huguenot
rising, and in the Midi Damville remained
unchallenged. On 5 February 1576, Henri de
Navarre fled the court. Reverting to his
Protestant faith, he retired to his domain in
the south-west and began raising an army.
On 9 April Alençon declared  that he
intended to win by force the peace which he
had failed to achieve by reason. Henry III's
response was once again to call on his
mother's help. She met Alençon and other
Malcontents at Chastenoy, near Sens. The
result was the Edict of Beaulieu (6 May)
which became known as the 'Peace of

Monsieur' because everyone believed that it
had been forced on the king by Alençon,
who, as the king's brother, had the title of
'Monsieur'. For the first time, the Huguenots
gained freedom of worship throughout
France except in Paris or at court. They were
allowed access to all professions, hospitals
and schools. Courts including judges of both
religions were to be set up in all parlements.
The massacre of St Bartholomew was
condemned as a crime and its victims
rehabilitated. Eight security towns were
conceded to the Huguenots in Languedoc,
Guyenne, Dauphiné and Provence, and a
meeting of the Estates-General was to be
called within six months. Secret clauses
rewarded the Malcontents. Alençon assumed
the title of duc d'Anjou; Condé and Damville
resumed their governorships of Picardy and
Languedoc respectively; John Casimir became
duc d'Étampes, and Navarre's governorship of
Guyenne was extended to Poitou and
Angoumois. But the edict did not rid France of
John Casimir's army. Henry III's finance
minister, Bellièvre, made frantic efforts to
satisfy John Casimir's exorbitant terms. On
5 July it was agreed that the reiters would leave
on receipt of two months' pay, and six French
noblemen were handed over as hostages.

## The sixth war (December 1576 – September 1577)

The Peace of Monsieur provoked widespread Catholic indignation. Placards denouncing it appeared all over Paris and Henry III had to force through its registration by the Parlement. Defensive associations suddenly reappeared. Outside Paris, Picardy took the lead in opposing the peace. Jacques

d'Humières, the governor of Péronne, begged the king not to hand over the province to

In 1584 a Catholic League was formed to exclude the Protestant leader, Henri de Navarre, from the throne. Even after becoming King Henry IV in 1589, he had to fight the League led by Mayenne and assisted by Spain. He was victorious only after converting to Catholicism.
**1.** 20/10/1587    **4.** 21/09/1589
**2.** 26/10/1587    **5.** 14/13/1590
**3.** 24/11/1587    **6.** 05/06/1595

The last wars 1585–1598

**Nantes** Treaty or edict
*GUISE* Governor
◨ Siege
Huguenot France
Under control of the League
Catholic areas under control of the King

ENGLAND

Calais

SPANISH NETHERLANDS

Arques   Amiens   **Vervins**

◻Rouen

ELBOEUF   Ivry ⚔   ◻PARIS   *GUISE*

MERCŒUR

Chartres○  ⚔ Auneau

**Nemours**

⚔ Vimory

LORRAINE

Blois   Fontaine   FRANCHE
Tours   Français ⚔   COMTE

**Nantes**

SWITZERLAND

La Rochelle   F R A N C E   Geneva

*MATIGNON*

SAVOY

Bordeaux○   ⚔ Coutras

Toulouse

JOYEUSE   EPERNON

N

S P A I N

0          100 miles
0          200 km

Condé. One hundred and fifty noblemen rallied to his support. At the same time an organisation, known as the League of Péronne, was set up with the aim of ensuring that the town and province remained Catholic. A manifesto proposed the establishment of a militia and links with like-minded nobles in other provinces. Within a short time the League became almost nation-wide, as noblemen in several provinces raised funds and gathered troops to defend the Catholic faith. Henry III found himself in a precarious situation as he himself regarded the recent peace as a humiliation. He looked to the Estates-General which met at Blois in November to provide him with the means to reassert his authority. As the Huguenots had been virtually excluded from the elections to the estates, the king could expect support. The majority of deputies opposed the recent peace. The king, meanwhile, tried to take the sting out of the League of Péronne and similar associations by setting up a league of his own. On 2 December he sent to all provincial governors a deed of association for their signature. An armed force was to be set up in each province and funds raised for its upkeep. By making himself head of the Catholic League, Henry III hoped to reassert his authority and dissuade Catholic extremists from acting independently.

In the meantime, a majority of deputies in the Estates-General voted for the restoration of religious unity throughout the kingdom. This suited the king, who needed an excuse to break the peace, and on 3 January 1577 he declared that he could no longer accept two religions in his kingdom and intended to eradicate heresy. Lacking the means to fight a new war, he looked to the Estates-General to vote new taxes, but aside from the clergy, who granted him a paltry sum, they failed to do so. An audit commission blamed Henry III's fiscal plight on his own extravagance. On 1 March he informed his council that, given the estates' attitude, he had little hope of restoring religious unity. But he did succeeed in detaching Damville from the Huguenots. The governor of Languedoc renewed his allegiance, weakening the Huguenots, who had begun

re-arming in Poitou and Guyenne. In spite of the estates' unhelpful attitude, Henry III did manage to raise a new army. It was made up of 20 companies of gendarmerie, 60 of infantry, 18 cannon, six smaller guns and sufficient powder and shot for 10,000 discharges. But he could only afford to keep it in the field for one month. Anjou was appointed to lead it, but the real commander was the duc de Nevers. On 25 April 1577 the army laid siege to La Charité-sur-Loire. The town surrendered on 2 May and was sacked. Anjou was given a hero's welcome when he returned to court. On 28 May he rejoined the army (by now only about 5,000 strong) as it besieged Issoire in Auvergne. Although the town's governor was warned of the dire consequences of resistance, he put up a brave fight, and Henry III ordered his brother to punish Issoire for its disobedience. Anjou complied by sacking the town mercilessly after its surrender on 12 June. Meanwhile, Nevers was complaining that he no longer had any ammunition, as his troops dragged themselves through the Limousin, and Henry III admitted that his treasury was empty. The war was far from won, yet Nevers and his army were recalled. Despite the loss of La Charité and Issoire, the Huguenots retained several strongholds in the south, and Navarre and Condé were still at large with their forces. When they captured Brouage on the Atlantic coast and began receiving aid from England, Henry III decided to come to terms. Peace was signed at Bergerac on 14 September. Although the settlement seriously curtailed freedom of Protestant worship, it gave the kingdom eight years of respite, apart from a brief lapse in 1579–1580. Henry III used the peace to shore up his authority.

## The seventh war (November 1579 – November 1580)

France was officially at peace from 17 September 1577, yet the reality, especially in the south, was closer to anarchy. It became normal for the independent nobleman with his own troops to wage war in his private interest, and large-scale peasant revolts broke out in Vivarais and the Dauphiné. Peasant unrest often assumed the character of a class conflict rather than a religious war–for example, a popular rising at Romans in 1579 was primarily a protest against the aristocratic privilege of tax exemption. At the same time nobles fought each other in various parts of France. On 28 February 1579 Catherine de' Medici signed a treaty at Nérac with the Huguenots. The situation in the south remained precarious, but it was in the north that the seventh religious war broke out. It has been blamed on Marguerite de Valois's amorous intrigues (hence its nickname of 'the Lovers' War'), but in fact it resulted largely from Catholic resistance to Condé becoming governor of Picardy. Condé accused the duc d'Aumale of trying to revive the Picard League and, in November 1579, seized the town of La Fère. It was recaptured in September 1580 by Marshal Matignon.  Fighting also broke out in the south where Henri de Navarre stormed Cahors. Yet the war did not develop into a major conflict because many Huguenots kept a low profile. Except in a few places, Languedoc as a whole remained calm, and in November 1580 Anjou negotiated the peace of Fleix, which allowed the Huguenots to keep their security towns for a further six years.

## The eighth war (September 1585 – April 1598)

The last of the French Wars of Religion was prompted by a succession crisis. King Henry III had no son. His younger brother and heir presumptive, François duc d'Anjou, died on 10 June 1584, leaving the path to the throne clear for the next in line, who was Henri de Navarre. As a Protestant, he was unacceptable to the majority of Catholics, who in the eighth war strove to exclude him from the throne. In September 1584 Henri de Guise and his brothers (the duc de Mayenne and the cardinal de Guise) formed an association at Nancy aimed at keeping Navarre off the throne. On 31 December they enlisted Spanish help through the Treaty of Joinville, under the terms of which King Philip II of Spain agreed

to subsidise an armed rising. Many nobles joined the rising, including Nevers, Brissac and most of the followers of the late duc d'Anjou, and military operations began at once. After raising troops in Champagne in March 1585, Guise captured Chalon, while Mayenne seized Dijon, Mâcon and Auxerre. As governors of Champagne and Burgundy respectively, they rallied their clients and set about recruiting more. In Brittany, Normandy and Picardy, other members of the Guise family – Mercoeur, Elbeuf and Aumale – stirred up trouble. Soon much of northern France was under Guise control. On 30 March the Leaguers published a manifesto at Péronne justifying their revolt. While standing up for the Catholic faith, they expressed the fear of being excluded from royal favour should a Protestant gain the throne. They were also deeply resentful of the favours that Henry III was showering on Anne duc de Joyeuse and Jean-Louis duc d'Épernon. Lacking the means to oppose the League, Henry once again looked to his mother to extricate him from his plight. She entered into talks with Guise, but he merely strung her along while building up his forces. Early in June, Catherine reported that Aumale's troops had occupied villages around Reims. She estimated that Guise had 25,000 men and 2,000 horses, excluding the forces of Elbeuf, Brissac and others. On 7 July Henry III effectively capitulated to the League. In the treaty of Nemours he promised to pay the troops which had been raised against him and conceded a number of security towns to the Leaguers, the lion's share going to Guise.

On 18 July 1585 the king banned Protestant worship and ordered all pastors to leave the kingdom. Their flocks were to abjure within six months or go into exile. Huguenots were debarred from all public offices and were to hand over the security towns in their possession, and Navarre was excluded from the throne. On 10 August he and Condé met Damville and renewed their alliance. In a joint manifesto, they accused the Guises of trying to seize the throne and, while affirming their loyalty to the crown, explained that they had no choice but to fight. On 7 October, Henry III branded them as traitors. He told the clergy he

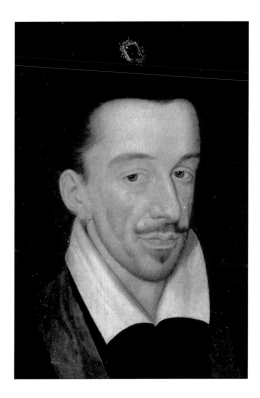

Henry III (1551–1589), King of France (1574–1589). The most intelligent of Henry II's three sons and a would-be reformer, he alienated most of his subjects by his aloofness, his blatant favouritism and his eccentric religious practices. As duc d'Anjou, he led the royal armies against the Huguenots, winning the battles of Jarnac and Moncontour, but failed to capture La Rochelle in 1572. He was elected King of Poland in 1573, but returned to France a year later following the death of his brother Charles IX. He soon had to face the bitter hostility of the Catholic League led by Henri duc de Guise and made the fatal mistake of having him assassinated at Blois in 1588. He was besieging Paris with the Huguenot leader, Henri de Navarre, in 1589 when he was himself assassinated by a fanatical Jacobin friar, Jacques Clément. This portrait by François Quenel is at the Louvre. (AKG, Berlin)

needed four armies to fight the Huguenots, and that these troops would cost 2 million *livres* per month. The clergy reluctantly agreed to sell church lands worth 50,000 crowns per annum, and the pope agreed to a further alienation worth 100,000 crowns, but war began before any of this money could reach the royal coffers. Early in March 1586, the king gave Guise command of 50 companies of infantry and between 5,000 and 6,000 cavalry. Another royal army, under Marshal d'Aumont, was sent to Auvergne and Languedoc, while Biron fought Condé in the west. Yet Henry III showed no inclination to fight seriously. He again asked his mother to negotiate, but the leaders of the League rejected in advance any settlement and agreed to act independently of the king. In the meantime, Elizabeth I of England offered Navarre money with which John Casimir, regent of the Palatinate, raised an army of 8,000 reiters to assist the Huguenots. Henry III had lost control of his kingdom. While Guise himself besieged Sedan and Jametz, towns belonging to the duc de Bouillon, Aumale captured others in Picardy. In August 1587 John Casimir's army,

consisting of 4,000 reiters, 3,000 landsknechts, 12,000 Swiss and 2,300 men under Bouillon, invaded the duchy of Lorraine. Overall command was entrusted to baron Fabian von Dohna. From Lorraine, the army entered Champagne, where it was joined by Protestant troops from Languedoc. Meanwhile, Henry III sent Joyeuse to fight Navarre in the west with an army of 6,000 foot and 2,000 horse. After gathering more troops at Saumur, he moved into Poitou at the end of July. Navarre's army being too small to risk a battle, he retreated to the safety of La Rochelle. Joyeuse overran Poitou, putting to the sword entire Huguenot garrisons, but disease and desertion soon caused his army to disintegrate. On 15 August he returned to Paris, leaving the remnants of his army in Touraine under his camp-master, Lavardin. Emerging from La Rochelle with 200 horse and 300 arquebusiers, Navarre pursued Lavardin to Chinon, but lacked the artillery needed to dislodge him. He did, however, reconquer Poitou in less than a fortnight.

On 12 September Henry III left Paris to join Épernon's army. He took up a position at Gien on the Loire with the aim of preventing Dohna's Germans from linking up with Navarre. Meanwhile Joyeuse raised a new army at Tours before resuming operations in Poitou. Exactly what Navarre planned at this stage is unclear. The royal offensive seems to have taken him by surprise. He hoped that Dohna's army would take some of the pressure off him, but the Germans soon tired of long marches. Their supplies were also running out. On finding Henry III at Gien, they decided to push along the right bank of the Loire towards Tours and Saumur. Navarre's army was too small to risk a confrontation with the king's forces. With the onset of winter, he fell back on Guyenne where he planned to raise more troops and to join forces with Damville. Joyeuse tried to intercept him, but Navarre managed to slip past. On 20 October Joyeuse attacked. Though not particularly well placed, Navarre accepted the challenge, and the rival armies faced each other outside Coutras. They were roughly equal in size: each had between 4,000 and 5,000 infantry. The Huguenots had 1,200 to 1,500 cavalry, and Joyeuse 1,500 to 1,800, but the Huguenots were hardened veterans, while Joyeuse's cavalry was made up of inexperienced young nobles anxious to show their valour. Before battle was joined, the Huguenots offered up prayers and sang the 118th Psalm. Their guns then opened fire, wreaking havoc among Joyeuse's infantry. The Royalist cavalry charged, only to give way at several points to a counter-charge by Navarre's horse. Joyeuse and his brother Claude were killed in the action as some of their comrades fled. After the

two-hour battle, 2,000 royalists lay dead on the field, including 300 nobles. According to Mornay, the Huguenots lost only two petty nobles and barely 30 men. Meanwhile Dohna's army, which had advanced into Beauce, began to fall apart. The reiters set off on their own, only to be twice defeated by Guise: once at Vimory on 26 October, then at Auneau on 24 November. The Swiss came to terms with Henry III. They agreed to go home in return for four months' pay. On 8 December the Germans agreed to depart in return for cash and under a strong escort. Guise, who had hoped to annihilate them on their return through Lorraine, felt cheated. Henry III returned to Paris in triumph on 23 December, but nothing could hide the fact that the real victors were his enemies: Guise and the League on the one hand, Navarre and the Huguenots on the other.

Henry III now provoked the League's fury by giving Épernon offices previously held by Joyeuse, including the governorship of

On 29 October 1587 a royalist army led by Henry III's favourite, Anne de Joyeuse, was heavily defeated on the plain of Coutras, near Bordeaux, by a Huguenot force under Henri de Navarre whose first major battle this was.

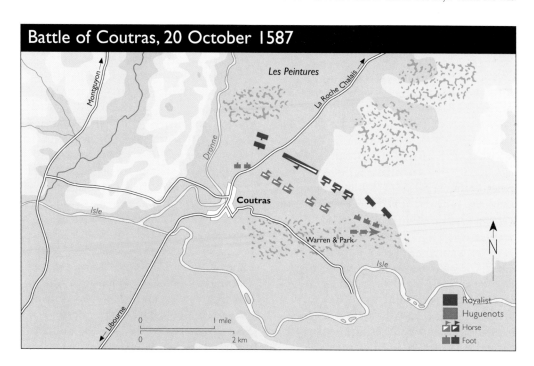

**Battle of Coutras, 20 October 1587**

Battle of Coutras (20 October 1587). This event marked a return to pitched battles after 18 years of sieges and skirmishes. Being anxious to prevent the Huguenots from receiving reinforcements from eastern France, Henry III encamped at Gien while ordering his favourite, the duc de Joyeuse, to fight Henry, King of Navarre. As Joyeuse advanced through Poitou, Navarre pushed into Périgord from La Rochelle. The two armies, which were of roughly equal size, collided near Coutras. In the action that followed the Huguenot pistols proved more effective than Royalist lances. Joyeuse fought bravely but was killed. More than 2,000 royal troops were killed, including some 300 nobles. Protestant losses were insignificant, but Navarre failed to follow up his victory. Instead of conquering towns in Poitou and Saintonge, he retired to Béarn in the south. (Ann Ronan Picture Library)

Normandy. Guise had wanted this governorship as his reward for defeating the Germans. Early in 1588 he and other Leaguers met at Nancy and addressed a number of demands to the king, including Épernon's dismissal from the government. Guise overran the duchy of Bouillon and blockaded Sedan, while Aumale tried to stir up trouble for Épernon in Normandy. Tension between Henry III and Guise exploded in May, when the duke accepted an invitation from the Sixteen, a revolutionary

body which controlled the Parisian League, in defiance of a royal ban. Henry reacted by introducing troops into the capital, thereby contravening its traditional right of self-defence. A mob poured into the streets, erected barricades and attacked the king's troops. Guise managed to quell the mob but on 13 May, Henry III fled to Chartres. Catherine de' Medici wanted him to capitulate to the League rather than face catastrophe. On 16 July Henry signed the Edict of Union: he dismissed Épernon, confirmed the treaty of Nemours, recognised the cardinal de Bourbon as heir-presumptive, bestowed more governorships on the Guises and appointed the duke as lieutenant-general of the kingdom. But, taking no chances, the Parisian League took steps to defend the capital against a possible royal attack. Its distrust was justified, for Henry III longed to avenge his humiliation. Early in September he summoned a meeting of the Estates-General at Blois only to find that most of the deputies favoured the League. On 23 December, Guise was lured to the king's chamber in the château and brutally murdered by Henry III's personal bodyguard. Next day the duke's brother, the cardinal de Guise, was also murdered and the cardinal de Bourbon, the League's candidate for the throne, was imprisoned. The king's action, far from strengthening his authority, plunged the kingdom into a new crisis. A frenzy of support for the League swept the country, bringing many more towns into its fold. Guise's brother, Charles duc de Mayenne assumed leadership of the movement. Nowhere was the reaction to the Blois murders more violent than in Paris, where Henry III was denounced by preachers as a new Herod. Pamphlets exalted the Guises as martyrs. A new revolutionary body was set up, which on 7 January 1589 released Frenchmen from their allegiance to the King and called on them to rise under arms. On 12 February Mayenne entered the capital at the head of an army and was appointed Lieutenant-general of the kingdom by the Sixteen. When Catherine de' Medici died on 5 January 1589, Henry III found himself alone, sandwiched between the League in the north and the Huguenots in the south. He controlled only a few towns and was

desperately short of money. Only by allying with Navarre could he hope to survive. On 30 April they signed an accord and, combining their forces, marched on the capital.  Henry III pitched camp at Saint-Cloud, but on 1 August he was assassinated by a fanatical friar who had come out of Paris supposedly to deliver a message to him. News of the king's death was greeted with jubilation in Paris. Catholic extremists assumed that the last obstacle in the path of a Catholic triumph had been removed.

Before dying, Henry III recognised Henri de Navarre as his heir, but many Catholics would

The assassination of King Henry III (1 August 1589). Contemporary woodcut. In July 1589 Henry III and the Huguenot leader, Henri de Navarre, laid siege to Paris. The king was residing at Saint-Cloud, when a Jacobin friar, Jacques Clément, asked to see him, saying that he was carrying important letters from the beleaguered capital. He was admitted to the king's presence, but, as Henry read one of the letters, Clément stabbed him in the lower abdomen. Seizing the knife, the king struck his assailant in the face and his courtiers cut him down. But the king's wound proved fatal. He died on 2 August after recognising Navarre as his heir and urging him to become a Catholic. (Ann Ronan Picture Library)

HENRY de Valloys grand Tiran de la France,
Voulant mettre a feu & fang de Paris les Catholiques
Par le confeil de fes faux fuppofts & heretiques
Se met en campagne pour les mettre en fouffrance
Mais Dieu par fa mifericorde & bonte,
Les a deliurez de fa tirannie & cruaute.

FRere Iaques Clement (Iacobin) homme de bien
Defirant veoir l'Eglife & le Peuple en repos
Se met en bon eftat & deuoir (comme bon chreftien)
Luy prefente vne lettre, & le tue fur ce propos
D'vn coufteau, fans auoir de perfonne accez,
Affin que puiffions viure en paix cy apres

not accept a Protestant king. The League, of course, remained resolutely hostile to Henry IV and acclaimed the cardinal de Bourbon as 'King Charles X' although he was still a prisoner. Henry managed to win over some of the captains who had been with Henry III at Saint-Cloud by making various promises. He undertook to seek instruction in the Catholic

On 21 September 1589 the armies of King Henry IV and of Charles duc de Mayenne, leader of the Catholic League, collided outside Arques in Normandy. The king and his cavalry stood between two trenches. Mayenne ordered his German foot to outflank the first ditch. While the infantry defending it fell back in confusion, Mayenne's cavalry charged, but the Swiss defending the second trench stood firm. As a morning mist lifted, the guns of Arques castle opened fire, forcing Mayenne to withdraw.

faith and to call a meeting of the Estates-General. Even so, many of the late king's followers, including Épernon and Nevers, deserted rather than serve a Protestant monarch. The royal army besieging Paris had meanwhile dwindled in size from 40,000 men to 18,000. With so few men Henry IV had to lift the siege. Outside the Protestant areas of the Midi only seven large towns supported him. Though urged by his captains to retire south of the Loire, he chose to go to Normandy in the expectation of English help. Mayenne pursued him there, promising either to throw him into the sea or to bring him back to Paris in chains. On reaching Dieppe, on 26 August 1589, Henry IV began fortifying the town. Moving slowly as usual, Mayenne

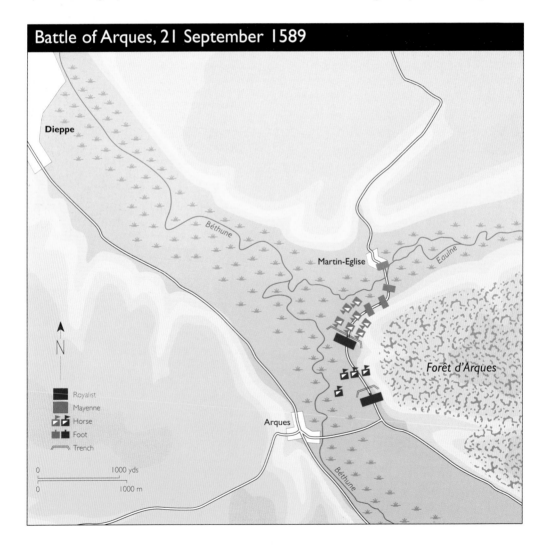

Battle of Arques, 21 September 1589

Dieppe

Béthune

Martin-Eglise

Eaulne

N

Forêt d'Arques

Royalist
Mayenne
Horse
Foot
Trench

0            1000 yds
0            1000 m

Arques

Béthune

reached Dieppe on 13 September. He hoped
to force a crossing at Arques, which was
defended by two parallel trenches covered by
the guns of the local castle. The two armies
were unevenly matched: Mayenne had
4,000 cavalry and 20,000 infantry; Henry IV
1,000 cavalry and 4,000 infantry. Battle was
joined on 21 September. As Mayenne's
infantry outflanked Henry's first trench, the
soldiers holding it fell back in confusion,
whereupon the duke's cavalry charged
through them. A furious battle ensued but the
Swiss, holding Henry's second trench, stood
firm. As the morning mist lifted, the guns of
Arques castle opened fire, inflicting such
grievous losses on Mayenne's army that he
had to withdraw. Henry now received help

A nineteenth-century engraving depicting the battle of
Arques (21 September 1589) between the armies of
King Henry IV and of Charles duc de Mayenne, the
leader of the Catholic League. Though Henry's army was
numerically inferior, he was helped by the terrain which
did not allow Mayenne to deploy his army to its full
strength. We see here a stage in the battle when the
guns of Arques castle opened fire on the Leaguers,
forcing them to withdraw. (Roger-Viollet)

and money from England as well as
reinforcements from southern France.
With an army 18,000 strong, he marched
on Paris. As suburb after suburb fell, Henry's
troops plundered them with impunity.
Meanwhile, Mayenne, who had returned
to the capital, set about refurbishing its
fortifications.

Lacking artillery, Henry was obliged to fall back, and shortage of money obliged him to disband part of his troops. After storming Vendôme on 20 November, he took over the administration which Henry III had set up at Tours after his flight from Paris in 1588. On 10 December he captured Laval, where he was joined by Breton reinforcements. After joining Biron at Alençon, the king resumed his campaign in Normandy, which attracted him, not only on account of its proximity to England, but also as the richest province in France. He hoped that it might provide him with much-needed funds. But Mayenne had rebuilt his forces and began regaining lost ground. Hearing that he was besieging Meulan, Henry laid siege to Dreux, and when Mayenne went to its relief, Henry

The accord sealed between King Henry III and the Huguenot leader, Henri de Navarre at Pléssis-les-Tours on 30 April 1589. On 12 May 1588 Henry III was forced to leave Paris which had fallen under the control of the Catholic League, led by Charles duc de Mayenne. Finding himself alone between the League's forces in the north and east of France, and those of the Huguenots in the south, he decided to ally with Henri de Navarre. They signed a truce on 26 April 1589, sealed it at Pléssis-les-Tours four days later, then jointly laid siege to Paris. (Roger-Viollet)

retreated along the Eure valley. On 13 March 1590 he drew up his army at Ivry near Evreux: six cavalry squadrons in line with some infantry screening them in front and other infantry between them. The guns were roughly in the centre and Biron commanded a small reserve behind. The disposition of Mayenne's army was similar. Once again, Henry's army was numerically inferior: 3,000 horse and 8,000 foot as against Mayenne's 5,000 horse and 12,000 foot, but the king's men had the advantage of having the sun behind them. He urged them to follow the white plume (*panache blanc*) on his hat if they lost sight of their standards. That way, he said, lay victory and honour. As the guns on both sides opened fire, the two bodies of cavalry collided. The struggle seemed more or less equal until Henry's cavalry broke through Mayenne's. A flanking charge by Biron's reserve carried the day. Ivry was essentially a cavalry action. Unlike Mayenne's men-at-arms who favoured the cumbersome lance, Henry's practised the *pistolade*, a tactic allegedly invented by him. His men would close in on the enemy before discharging their pistols and would then charge using their swords. Ivry was a great

Engraved portrait of Charles de Lorraine, duc de Mayenne (1554–1611), who became leader of the Catholic League following the assassination of his elder brother, Henri, third duc de Guise. The League had been set up to oppose the succession to the throne of a Protestant prince of the blood, namely Henri de Navarre. Mayenne continued to oppose him after he had become King Henry IV, but when the latter converted to Catholicism, Mayenne followed the example of many towns, including Paris, by submitting to him in January 1596. He had to give up the governorship of Burgundy, which he had held for 22 years, but became governor of Ile-de-France instead. Henry IV also agreed to take upon himself his war debts. (Roger-Viollet)

victory for Henry IV. Six thousand Leaguers were killed and thousands more taken prisoner. Forty standards were captured along with guns and a huge quantity of baggage.

No one knows what Henry IV now had in mind. Mayenne's army was no more and Paris lay virtually defenceless only 36 miles away. Yet Henry chose to linger for a fortnight at Mantes. When eventually he did move, he embarked on a leisurely curve of conquest through Corbeil, Melun, Provins, Bray-sur-Seine and Montereau, coming to a halt at Sens. He then set about blockading Paris. As his army was too small to encircle the capital, he tried to cut off its supplies by seizing a number of bridges over the Seine. Experience had taught him that it was a mistake to attack

Paris from the south, as this allowed the defenders to receive reinforcements from the north where the League was strongest. So Henry established his headquarters on the hill of Montmartre to the north of the capital. At the same time, he stationed troops in neighbouring villages. His artillery was positioned within range of the city. Mayenne, meanwhile, rebuilt his forces, amassing 1,500 landsknechts and as many Swiss and arquebusiers. He also had the urban militia totalling 48,000 men. Henry IV's army was comparatively small, numbering no more than 20,000. The siege of Paris, which lasted from 7 May until 30 August, inflicted terrible hardships on the inhabitants. Some 13,000 of the 30,000 victims of the siege allegedly died of hunger. As public morale faltered, preachers exhorted the people to face death rather than peace under a heretical monarch. Huge processions were organised as demonstrations of religious zeal and solidarity. One of these, on 14 May, consisted of monks and friars armed with arquebuses, halberds and daggers. Any backsliding was harshly punished by the Sixteen. The siege was accompanied by a wave of searches and arrests leading to fines, imprisonment or death. One foreign observer who feared that Paris might fall into Protestant hands was the king of Spain, Philip II. He ordered Alexander Farnese, duke of Parma (his commander in the Low Countries) to invade northern France with 14,000 Spanish veterans. On 23 August Parma was joined at Meaux by Mayenne with 10,000 foot and 2,000 horse. Henry IV's army was almost as large, having recently received reinforcements from southern France. Henry withdrew some troops from Paris and faced Parma at Chelles, but Parma refused battle. Instead, a force of Spaniards unblocked one supply-route to Paris by capturing Lagny. On 9 September Henry IV retreated. He split up his army into four parts and sent them to Touraine, Champagne, Normandy and Burgundy, leaving only a rump near Paris. On 22 September Parma laid siege to Corbeil. After the town's fall, on 16 October, he returned to the Low Countries, leaving

## Battle of Ivry, 14 March 1590

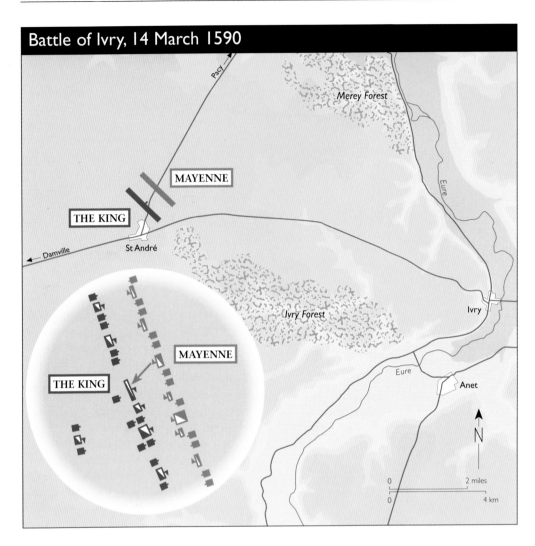

On 13 March 1590 King Henry IV inflicted a heavy defeat at Ivry, near Dreux, on the army of the Catholic League commanded by Charles duc de Mayenne.

Mayenne in charge of the League's forces. Shortage of cash forced Henry IV to disband all his mercenaries, save the Swiss. His only asset at this stage was the split in the League between the Parisian radicals and Mayenne's noblemen. Excesses committed by the Sixteen in Paris forced Mayenne to intervene. He occupied the capital on 28 November 1591, ending the rule of the radicals. Henceforth, Henry IV only had to face Mayenne's League.

Instead of attacking Rouen, the League's main stronghold in northern France, Henry IV now chose to capture Chartres, then Noyon, tightening his partial blockade of Paris. The terms of Noyon's surrender included an indemnity of 40,000 crowns, which helped him pay his troops. On 29 September he inspected at Vandy, near Verdun, an army which Turenne had raised for him in Germany. Meanwhile, Elizabeth I of England offered him troops on condition that he would attack Rouen. Her offer seems to have impressed the king. After hovering between Paris and Chartres, he suddenly swung westwards and captured Louviers. He informed Elizabeth that he was ready to oblige her. In August an expeditionary force under the Earl of Essex landed at Dieppe, and on 11 November 1591 Biron laid siege to Rouen. Rouen was defended by the sieur de

ABOVE Henry IV at the battle of Ivry. As a Protestant, Henry IV had to fight his way to the throne. His path was blocked by the Catholic League led by Charles, duc de Mayenne. On 14 March 1590 the rival armies collided at Ivry, near Evreux. The action that followed was essentially a cavalry engagement and gave Henry a chance to display his best fighting qualities. It was on this occasion that he famously told his men that they would find honour by following the white plume (*panache blanc*) adorning his hat. Painting by Peter Paul Rubens. Musée Bonnat, Bayonne. (AKG, Berlin)

BELOW The relief of Paris by the duke of Parma (1590). Mural by Rodrigo de Holanda in the Sala de las Batallas at the Escorial, near Madrid. Paris was besieged several times during the eighth religious war. The worst siege lasted from May till September 1590 when the capital was hit by famine. On 7 September, however, a strong and well-disciplined Spanish army commanded by Alessandro Farnese duke of Parma seized Ligny, thereby ending the blockade of Paris by opening up the river Marne to traffic. (AKG, Berlin)

Barnabé Brisson (1531–1591), first president of the
Parlement of Paris. He was not only a distinguished
lawyer, but also a most learned man whom Henry III
held in the highest regard. A zealous Catholic, he chose
to remain in Paris after the king had been forced to leave
by the League. Brisson, however, fell foul of Catholic
extremists who, in the absence of Mayenne, instituted
a regime of terror in the capital. On 15 November 1591
they burst into the Parlement and seized Brisson and
two of his fellow magistrates. Without so much as a trial,
they hanged them from a beam in the courtroom of the
Petit Châtelet. Thus did Brisson achieve a posthumous
fame which might have eluded him otherwise.
(Ann Ronan Picture Library)

Villars, who took steps to repair the town's
fortifications, brought guns from Le Havre
and reinforced the 6,000-strong garrison.
Henry IV joined Biron and Essex on
23 November. They concentrated their
efforts on taking Fort Sainte-Catherine but
were repeatedly thrown back. Essex was so
discouraged that he returned to England in
January 1592. The morale of the defenders
was continually boosted by religious
processions and sermons reminding them of
divine support for their cause, but their main

hope lay with Parma. In November he inspected 16,000 troops at Valenciennes and on 28 December joined Mayenne and Guise. Parma occupied La Fère, hoping to use it as his base. On 18 January he commanded 13,546 infantry and 4,061 cavalry. As he pressed on towards Rouen, he marshalled his army in a close and protective formation. Fearing a repetition of what had happened in Paris, Henry IV left all his infantry with Biron outside Rouen and set off himself with 7,000 cavalry to harass the duke. The rival armies met on 3 February 1592 on the Bresle, a small river dividing Picardy from Normandy. Henry rashly led a cavalry charge against Parma's cavalry only to be cut off from his base. The king was slightly wounded in the action and some 60 of his nobles were killed.

While Henry recovered from his wound at Dieppe, Parma seized Neufchâtel before resuming his march on Rouen. On 24 February, Villars launched a fierce attack on Biron's entrenchments. The marshal was wounded and forced to retire to Darnétal. The way seemed clear for Parma to enter Rouen, but he was dissuaded by Mayenne who did not want the city to become a Spanish stronghold outside his own control. After posting part of his army at Neufchâtel, Parma returned to Picardy with a large force and besieged Rue at the mouth of the Somme. By now Villars' resources were dwindling and the people of Rouen were clamouring for 'peace or bread'. Once Henry IV had rejoined Biron at Darnétal, they resumed the siege of Rouen. Villars warned Parma that without help he would be unable to hold out beyond 20 April. Responding quickly, Parma sent 5,000 horse and 12,000 foot, forcing Henry to draw his army back south of Rouen. On 21 April Parma and Mayenne entered the city in triumph. Its liberation, however, did not end the sufferings of the inhabitants. The neighbouring countryside had been

stripped bare by the besiegers who also brought with them infectious diseases. By early 1593 nearly three times as many people had been buried as in a normal year.

Parma now attacked Caudebec, a town blocking the road to Le Havre. This allowed Henry IV to rebuild his army. Many nobles who had gone home for the winter returned refreshed, and the king soon had an army of 8,000 cavalry and 18,000 infantry. He tried to trap Parma in the Pays de Caux between the Seine and the sea, but the duke arranged for boats and pontoons to be sent from Rouen to Caudebec and on the night of 21 May his army crossed the Seine at a point where the river was deemed impassable. By the time Henry IV reached the scene, the enemy had flown. Having crossed the Seine, Parma's army marched eastward at speed, reaching Saint-Cloud in five days. The duke reinforced the Spanish garrison in Paris before returning to the Low Countries. On 2 December, however, Parma died in Arras. Henry decided to give up serious campaigning for the time being. He disbanded his army and set off with a flying force of 3,000 horse and 6,000 foot to Champagne, but arrived too late to save the town of Épernay, which fell to the League on 8 August. As the year 1592 ended Henry was no nearer to capturing Paris, without which he could not call the kingdom his own.

In the meantime, royalists and Leaguers fought each other in other parts of France. In the west, the duc de Mercoeur launched an offensive aimed at regaining Maine and Anjou from the king. A royal army was beaten off on 21 May as it tried to seize Craon. Elsewhere, the League were less successful. In Languedoc, they threatened Montauban after occupying Carcassonne, and planned to besiege Villemur (Guyenne), but were defeated on 20 October. In the south-east, the Protestant leader, Lesdiguières, tried to prevent the duke of Savoy from occupying Provence.

# Two soldier-writers, one Huguenot captain

## Blaise de Monluc

Blaise de Monluc was born in 1501 in Gascony, a province reputed to be fertile only in soldiers. His earliest experience of war was gained in the Italian Wars. In 1525 he was taken prisoner at Pavia, but soon released as he was not worth a ransom. Two years later he shared marshal Lautrec's defeat at Naples and was seriously wounded. In 1534 he served in one of Francis I's provincial legions and in the 1540s fought in Piedmont. Under King Henry II, he attached himself to the rising star of François duc de Guise, and in 1554 defended Siena, which had rebelled against its Florentine overlord. On returning to France, he was appointed colonel-general of the infantry and knighted. After the peace of Cateau-Cambrésis, however, he fell upon hard times. He thought of joining the Huguenots in south-west France, but decided that his interests would be better served by supporting the Catholic cause. As the king's lieutenant-general in Guyenne, he kept the peace for five years at the cost of much cruelty. Two executioners accompanied him everywhere, administering summary justice at his bidding. Monluc boasted that his passage through Guyenne could be easily plotted on a map thanks to the bodies which he left hanging from trees lining the roads. When a rebel leader at Saint-Mezard begged Monluc to spare his life, he seized the poor man by the throat, screaming: 'How dare you ask for mercy when you have disobeyed your king?' Throwing him down onto a stone cross, he had him instantly beheaded. The sword blow was so violent that part of the cross was broken off. At Fumel, in 1562, Monluc ordered 30 or 40 Huguenots to be hanged or broken on the wheel without trial. At Gironde, he ordered 80 prisoners of war to be hanged from pillars in the market hall. In September 1562 he was responsible for a massacre at Terraube. A deep well was filled to the top with bodies.

Cruelty was essential to the effective conduct of war, according to Monluc. His nights, on his own admission, were never peaceful: he was always fighting enemies in his sleep. Doctors blamed his imagination, but a guilty conscience was more probably to blame. Disfigured at the age of 70 by a shot from an arquebus, Monluc had to wear a mask for the rest of his days. On being relieved of his governorship, he turned to writing his memoirs, calling them *Commentaires* in imitation of Julius Caesar. The French Wars of Religion produced many military autobiographies. If their aristocratic authors felt uneasy about taking up the pen in place of the sword, they could take comfort from the example of Caesar, who had combined a brilliant military career with authorship. 'The greatest captain that ever lived', wrote Monluc, 'was Caesar, and he has shown me the way, having himself written his own commentaries, and being careful to record by night the actions he had performed by day'. Monluc wrote long after the events he described and his memory sometimes let him down. Writing, however, enabled him to relive his wartime experiences and also to impart lessons to his fellow-captains. He warned them against the perils of

OPPOSITE Blaise de Monluc (1500–1577), marshal of France. Monluc was born in Gascony, a region reputed to be fertile only in soldiers. It also provided literature with a type: the *cadet de Gascogne*, the best known being d'Artagnan and *Cyrano de Bergerac*. Like them, Monluc was brave and boastful. Having fought in the Italian Wars, he took a leading part in the Wars of Religion, fighting on the Catholic side. As governor of Guyenne, he kept the peace for five years at the cost of much bloodshed. At the age of 70, he was disfigured by an arquebus shot and forced to wear a mask for the rest of his life. On being relieved of his governorship, he became a lonely and embittered old man, but he wrote a wonderful set of memoirs, called *Commentaires*, after Julius Caesar whose example he tried to follow. (AKG, Berlin)

gambling, drink, avarice – 'and there is a fourth,' he wrote – 'it is the love of women. If you cannot avoid it, at least approach it soberly. Do not lose your head or commit yourself. That is the exact opposite of a stout heart. When Mars is campaigning, put aside love; you will have time enough for it later.'

Monluc thought artillery was more frightening than effective and shared Machiavelli's distrust of foreign mercenaries. Historical truth, he believed, could be found not in abstract speculation but in the smell of gunpowder and blood. Even so, like the proverbial Gascon, he was inclined to exaggerate and boast. The doctrinal issues dividing Catholics from Protestants did not interest him. The only religious test he understood was whether his faith was that of

the king. Viewing religion and politics as indivisible, Monluc refused to allow freedom of conscience precedence over obedience to the monarch. The first version of the *Commentaries* was dictated in 1570–1571 and the last in 1576. Monluc died, a lonely and embittered old man, in 1577.

## François de la Noue

François de La Noue was born in 1531. Though trained as a soldier, he was also well-read in the classical historians, Scriptures, Church Fathers and contemporary authors. Although he became a Protestant about 1559, he remained on good terms with the duc de Guise and was chosen to accompany Mary Stuart to Scotland in 1560. In the first religious war, he fought at Dreux under Condé. In the second, he lost an arm, which was replaced by an iron one – hence his nickname 'bras de fer'. In spite of his chosen career, La Noue hated war. He also deplored the divisions among his countrymen. In 1572 he fought in the Low Countries. Later, he was given the impossible

ABOVE The Château of Estillac-en-Agenais (Lot-et-Garonne). Situated seven km from Agen on high ground overlooking the Garonne river, this was the home of the famous Gascon soldier, Blaise de Monluc, who acquired a reputation for savagery during the religious wars. About 1570 he began fortifying his home in a radical way. Triangular in plan, it has two bastions at the eastern and southern angles which are based on designs by Italian military engineers. It was here that Monluc wrote his memoirs, called *Commentaires*, which Henry IV called 'the soldiers' Bible'. (Author's own collection)

task of persuading his co-religionists to surrender La Rochelle to the king, and instead took over command of the town's defences. After that he commanded the Huguenots in western France. In 1578 he followed the duc d'Alençon to the Low Countries, and in 1580 was taken prisoner by the Spaniards. It was during his captivity, which lasted five years, that he wrote his *Discours politiques et militaires*. This, unlike Monluc's *Commentaires*, is not an autobiography. La Noue's personal recollections form only the 26th part of his book; the rest being concerned with ethical, religious, political, economic and military matters. The *Discours* is a kind of encyclopaedia, intended to warn La Noue's fellow-nobles and soldiers of the perils facing

The Capture of Montbrison by the Des Adrets (June 1562). The French Wars of Religion witnessed atrocities on both sides. Des Adrets was the Protestant counterpart of Blaise de Monluc. He was allegedly responsible for many acts of cruelty though not all are reliably documented. The worst was the so-called 'jumping' (*sauterie*) of Montbrison when Des Adrets ordered prisoners of war to be thrown from a tall tower into a fire. (Ann Ronan Picture Library)

France and to point to the remedies available to them. La Noue believed that the army, like much else in France, had degenerated since his youth, its discipline especially having crumbled away. Two monsters, he claimed, were devouring France: *la picorée* (pillage) and massacre. He advocated a revival of the feudal levy and the creation of a standing army of 2,500 infantry. He was critical of the traditional way of disposing cavalry, favouring compact blocks instead. Regarding fortification, he thought earthworks were cheaper and more effective than the elaborate structures favoured by Italian military engineers. By saving money on one fortress, he wrote, 10 more could be built. But La Noue's memoirs range beyond military matters. They are remarkable especially for their tolerance and humanity. Thus he praises the duc de Guise for his courteous treatment of the prince de Condé after the battle of Dreux. As there were few beds left after the destruction of the prince's baggage, the victorious duke invited his defeated prisoner to share his own. 'It seems to me,' writes La Noue, 'that such fine deeds ought not to be forgotten so that those who follow the profession of arms may learn to imitate them and avoid the cruelties and base acts which many of them perpetrate because they do not know or do not wish to know how to curb their hatred.' It has been said that he did not know how to hate. He never forgot that Jesus died for all Christians, not just a few, and that all Frenchmen were brothers. The contrast between him and Monluc could not be greater.

## Baron des Adrets

François de Beaumont, baron des Adrets (1513–87) was a lesser nobleman from Dauphiné whose military career began in the Italian Wars. Having been captured by the Spaniards at Montcalvo, he was set free after paying a ransom which left him destitute. Like other veterans of the Italian Wars, he viewed the peace of Cateau-Cambrésis as a betrayal. He challenged the governor of

Montcalvo to a duel, but it was banned by the Guises who controlled the government of Francis II. This may have turned des Adrets into a Protestant. In the first religious war he fought under Condé, capturing Valence in April 1562 and some smaller towns. He committed atrocities allegedly in reprisal for Catholic excesses. In May the baron set up a veritable dictatorship in Lyon. He seized Grenoble in June after sacking the abbey of Saint Antoine, then captured Romans and Saint-Marcellin. At Montbrison, he allegedly ordered three or four hundred prisoners of war to be thrown off a tower into a burning brazier. Des Adrets was criticised for spreading his activities too widely instead of attending to the defence of Lyon. In July 1562 Condé appointed the seigneur de Soubise in his place. Early in 1563 des Adrets was arrested and taken to Nîmes for trial, only to be set free by the Peace of Amboise. Angered by Condé's snub, des Adrets decided to switch sides. In the second religious war, he besieged Mâcon (1567) and La Côte-Saint-André (1568) for the king. His admission to the order of St Michael suggests that he had reverted to being a Catholic. In 1569 he led 17 *enseignes* of Dauphiné to the duc d'Aumale in Lorraine, but on being suspected of corresponding secretly with the young Protestant princes of Condé and Navarre, he was arrested and imprisoned in Lyon. He was set free following the peace of Saint-Germain and Charles IX assured him that he had never doubted of his loyalty. Henry III, however, was less forthcoming when the baron called on him at Lyon in 1574. Des Adrets retired to the château of Romanesche, but in 1585, at the start of the eighth religious war, he returned to Lyon to give advice to the sieur de la Valette, who commanded the king's army. Des Adrets died in 1587. He is mainly remembered for his cruelty, although he claimed that he never broke the laws of war. Some of his misdeeds have not been proven, but he was certainly an unpleasant man who reacted violently to any offence, alleged or real. Religion seems not to have mattered greatly to him.

# The impact of the Wars of Religion on France's neighbours

A civil war by its very nature is confined to a single country, but its impact may reach out beyond that country's frontiers. This is all the more likely to happen if the war has a religious or ideological content which arouses the sympathy of foreigners. A recent example is the Spanish Civil War of the 1930s, which brought in volunteers from abroad in the form of the International Brigade to fight for the Republican cause, as well as military support for General Franco's Nationalists from Nazi Germany and Fascist Italy. A conflict of political ideologies was at stake here. The conflicts which tore France apart in the 16th century were not dissimilar – religion was a powerful divisive factor which found echoes in other European countries. Protestant powers like England, some German principalities and the Dutch rebels viewed with dismay the persecution of their co-religionists by the French monarchy and tried to assist them in various ways. Catholic powers, like Spain and the Papacy, were anxious to prevent France from falling into Protestant hands. The wars had another, less obvious, impact on Europe generally. Whereas the French monarchy had been a major political force on the international scene in the first half of the 16th century, invading Italy repeatedly and stirring up trouble for the Habsburg rulers of Spain and the Holy Roman Empire, the civil wars during the second half of the century effectively neutralised it. The King of Spain, Philip II, found himself free to dominate Italy and the western Mediterranean. As the leading champion of the Catholic cause in Europe, his private sympathies naturally lay with the Catholics in the French civil wars, and under the Treaty of Joinville he undertook to help the League led by the House of Guise. His ambassador in France, Bernardino de Mendoza, played a significant role in the Parisian League's opposition to King Henry III, but Philip II also wanted to prevent the French from assisting the rebels in the Netherlands. He had an interest in ensuring that civil strife continued in France for as long as possible and so did not support one side or the other too decisively.

Soon after the outbreak of the first religious war, Catherine de' Medici sought help from the pope, the duke of Savoy and Philip II of Spain. She told the English envoy, Sir Henry Sidney, that she would suppress Condé's revolt with Spanish help unless Condé accepted her peace terms. At first, the Huguenots were more interested in seeking the mediation of foreign princes than their financial or military aid. Admiral Coligny was reluctant to expose them to the charge of treason, but Huguenot policy changed once it became known that the crown had decided to ask Spain for military aid. While d'Andelot raised troops in Germany, two Huguenot agents sought help from Queen Elizabeth I of England. She did not allow religious sentiment to override her political interests. Her main concern was to regain Calais, which had been returned to France for eight years under the Treaty of Cateau-Cambrésis. She insisted on occupying Le Havre in return for a loan of 140,000 crowns. This was conceded by the Huguenots in the Treaty of Hampton Court and soon afterwards English troops occupied Le Havre which was to be exchanged for Calais before the eight years were up.

Some Frenchmen believed the religious divisions in France could best be healed by uniting the nation in a common struggle against the foreigner. The Peace of Amboise (March 1563) offered a chance to test this idea. Many Huguenots who had been unhappy about bringing English troops into France now tried to clear their consciences by helping Charles IX to reconquer Le Havre. A large army under the Constable Montmorency and marshal Brissac laid siege to the town. After a three-day bombardment, the garrison surrendered. The French government now argued that the English had forfeited all rights to Calais by their occupation of Le Havre. Months of wrangling ensued. Eventually, under the Treaty of Troyes (11 April 1564) France kept Calais in return for a payment of 120,000 crowns.

The Calvinist challenge to royal authority was not confined to France. It also manifested itself in the Low Countries where a serious rebellion broke out in 1566. Philip II of Spain, as we have seen, sent an army under the duke of Alba to restore order, but the rebellion continued. The Dutch Revolt gained support from several quarters, including England and France. The French government had enough troubles to deal with at home without seeking to antagonise Spain by assisting the Dutch rebels but individual Frenchmen, particularly Huguenots, tried to assist their Dutch co-religionists. In April 1568 the Spanish ambassador in France got wind of an alliance between the Huguenot leaders and the Dutch rebels, known as the 'Sea Beggars'. Philip II warned Charles IX that he risked losing his throne and his life if he did not cut off the heads of the Huguenot leaders. In the summer Marshal Cossé was ordered to prevent a force of Huguenots under Paul de Mouvans and François de Cocqueville from marching to Flanders to help the Dutch. He crushed them at Saint-Valéry and Catherine de' Medici ordered the marshal to execute his prisoners or send them to the galleys.

The desire of some Huguenots to assist the Dutch rebels was reciprocated but not always effectively. In November 1568 William prince of Orange led an army into France from Germany intending to join a Huguenot force in Poitou, but his troops were unpaid and poorly fed. With her son's army engaged elsewhere, Catherine de' Medici tried to buy off William, while Charles IX offered him free passage back to Germany. Fearing mutiny among his men,

William retreated across the Moselle in January 1569. In 1571, following the peace of Saint-Germain, the idea of a French military intervention to help the Dutch rebels was actively canvassed in France. While William of Orange prepared to invade the Netherlands from Germany, his brother Louis of Nassau and other Dutch exiles tried to organise another invasion from France. It seems that Charles IX, who was intensely jealous of the military successes of his brother the duc d'Anjou in the last civil war, was not averse to meddling in the Netherlands on his own account. In July 1571 he attended a secret meeting at the château of Lumigny at which a plan for the partition of the Netherlands between France, England and the Empire was considered, and in October he sanctioned an armed intervention by France in the Netherlands, but his mother, Catherine de' Medici (who was most anxious to avoid a war with Spain) got his decision rescinded. Even so, Nassau and his fellow exiles in France stepped up their preparations. In April 1572 the 'Sea Beggars' opened a new chapter in the Dutch Revolt by seizing the port of Brill. William of Orange declared war on Spain, and Nassau urged Charles IX to support the rebels, but the king felt unable to go against his mother's wishes. So Nassau acted alone. In May, he and some Huguenots seized the towns of Valenciennes and Mons. The Huguenot leader, Coligny, pressed Charles to assist them, but in vain. In June, Charles forbade his subjects to cross the Dutch border in aid of Nassau. But in July he allowed a small Huguenot army led by the seigneur de Genlis to go to the relief of Mons, which was being besieged by Alba. Charles disclaimed responsibility for the expedition, but Alba treated it as an act of war by France. The expedition was intercepted before it could reach Mons and decisively crushed. The Genlis fiasco underlined the need for Coligny to go to the aid of William of Orange in the Netherlands. He pointed to the dangers that would befall France in the event of Orange being defeated. Coligny indicated that the

Huguenots were becoming restless. The choice facing Charles IX, he claimed, was between war with Spain and a renewal of civil war in France. But the king's council refused to be dragged into war. Even so, a Huguenot army gathered near Mons, and Coligny gathered a substantial force. But on

Alessandro Farnese, third duke of Parma (1545–1592), the nephew of King Philip II of Spain. He succeeded Don John of Austria as governor general of the Netherlands in 1578 and fought the Dutch rebels led by William of Orange, regaining much ground from them in the southern Netherlands. Philip II called on him to assist the Spanish war effort against England and the Catholic League in northern France. In 1590 Parma relieved Paris which Henry IV was besieging. In April 1592 Henry tried to trap him in the Pays de Caux between the Seine and the Channel, but Parma extricated himself by a brilliant nocturnal manoeuvre. He reinforced the garrison in Paris before returning to the Netherlands, but died at Arras on 2 December of a wound he had suffered in Normandy. (Ann Ronan Picture Library)

22 August Coligny was shot and wounded in Paris and two days later he fell victim to the massacre of St Bartholomew. The Guises almost certainly were to blame for this, but some historians have also suspected Spanish and papal involvement. The Admiral's death ended any immediate prospect of the king of France assisting the Dutch rebels.

The urge to intervene in the Netherlands on the side of the Dutch rebels was not confined to the Huguenots. Spain was still regarded by certain members of the French nobility as the traditional enemy. Among them was François duc d'Alençon, who was jealous of the military successes of his elder brother, Henri, duc d'Anjou. The Netherlands seemed to offer him scope to compete on at least equal terms. The Dutch, for their part, were keen to enlist the support of a French prince of the blood. In February 1578 Alençon (who by now had become duc d'Anjou) fled from Henry III's court and began raising an army on his estates to assist the Dutch. On reaching Mons in July, he told William of Orange that he had come to help the Dutch Estates-General in their just quarrel with Spain, and a month later he signed a treaty with them. In exchange for his military assistance they appointed him 'Defender of the liberty of the Netherlands against the tyranny of the Spaniards and their allies'. This title, however, was meaningless. The Dutch did not wish to replace Spanish tyranny with a French one. The hopes they had placed in Anjou soon evaporated as his unpaid troops began to desert, ravaging the countryside.

The duc d' Anjou is best remembered in England as one of Elizabeth I's suitors. In the autumn of 1578 he made a new bid for her hand, but she indicated that she would never marry someone she had not met. Henry III and Catherine de' Medici accordingly urged him to visit England, if only to draw him away from the Low

Silver medal of Henry IV, King of Navarre (1572–1610) and of France (1589-1610). The son of Antoine de Bourbon, he became head of the Huguenot party after the death of his uncle, Condé, in 1569. He married Charles IX's sister, Marguerite, in 1572, but was kept a prisoner at court after the Massacre of St Bartholomew and forced to become a Catholic. After escaping, he reverted to his Protestant faith and led the Huguenot armies, fighting with distinction as a cavalry commander. He succeeded to the throne after Henry III's death in 1589 but had to overcome armed opposition from the Catholic League. He gained acceptance as king by again becoming a Catholic, but was assassinated in 1610. (Osprey Publishing)

Countries. After the Peace of Fleix in November 1580, Anjou hoped that Henry III would back his enterprise in the Low Countries with adequate funding, but Henry had no wish to become embroiled in a war with Spain, and gave his brother minimal support. In August Anjou seized Cambrai, but was soon driven back to the Channel coast. He visited England in October, but Elizabeth showed that she had no intention of marrying him. On returning to the Low Countries, Anjou assumed the title of duke of Brabant, but by October 1582 he was a desperate man and his attempt to seize Antwerp in January 1583 ended disastrously. He returned to France and died in June 1584, clearing the path to the throne for the Protestant leader Henri de Navarre.

The prospect of the crown of France falling into Protestant hands horrified King Philip II of Spain who was the principal secular champion of Catholicism in Europe. Although Henry III was still on the throne, Philip allowed his agents to sign the Treaty of Joinville in December 1584 with Henri, duc de Guise. In addition to recognising the cardinal de Bourbon as heir to the French throne, Philip promised in the Treaty to subsidise an armed rising by the League. After the assassination of Henry III in August 1589 and the accession of the Protestant leader, Henri de Navarre, as King Henry IV, foreign involvement in France's domestic affairs grew significantly. Elizabeth I offered Henry military support on condition that he concentrated his efforts on Normandy so that the Channel ports should not fall into

the hands of the League and Spain. She sent an expeditionary force under the Earl of Essex to help besiege Rouen. Philip II, for his part, ordered the duke of Parma (his commander in the Low Countries) to march to the relief of the town. After the death of the cardinal de Bourbon in May 1590, Philip put forward his daughter, the Infanta Isabella Clara Eugenia (the granddaughter of King Henry II of France) as a candidate for the French throne. But the Salic Law debarred women from the throne. Although some members of the Catholic League were prepared to consider her, the majority resented Spanish attempts to override one of France's cherished 'fundamental laws'. In June 1593 the Estates-General of the League firmly rejected the Infanta's candidature. But this did not mark the end of Spanish involvement in French affairs. In January 1595 Henry IV declared war on Spain in order to expel the remaining Spanish troops from France. After the Spaniards had been defeated in Burgundy, they captured a number of towns in northern France, including Amiens. Eventually, Henry IV recovered the lost ground and, in May 1598, he signed the Peace of Vervins with Spain. This did not meet with Elizabeth I's approval. She urged Henry to undermine Spanish power by assisting the Dutch rebels. Her words were not lost on him and from 1598 onwards he sent them substantial sums of money. Sometimes, too, he allowed French troops to be recruited to serve the Dutch cause. Such levies contravened the treaty of Vervins, but Henry ignored the Spanish protests. He also tried to foment trouble for Spain in the Mediterranean. In January 1601 he encouraged the Turks to attack the coast of Calabria and stirred up unrest among the Moriscos in Spain. But this 'cold war' was not one-sided. Spanish agents constantly promoted disloyalty among the French nobility. The English agent, Winwood, did not believe that real peace had ever existed between France and Spain since 1598. In his view each country was 'attending the opportunity who can first get the start on the other'.

# A lawyer, a surgeon, and a pastor

## Pierre de L'Estoile

Pierre de L'Estoile (1546–1611) is best remembered for the diary he kept during the Wars of Religion. He belonged to a family of jurists and magistrates. His father was a president in the Parlement of Paris and his mother the daughter of one of Francis I's Keepers of the Seals. As a child, he was taught by Mathieu Béroalde who became a Calvinist minister in Geneva. L'Estoile then studied law at Bourges. In 1569 he married Anne de Baillon, who gave him six children. After her death in 1580, he married Colombe Marteau, who gave him another 10 children. L'Estoile's huge family was to cause him many headaches and much expense. He became *grand audiencier* in the Parlement of Paris but little is known of his professional activities. He did not follow the king to Tours in 1589, but continued to serve the League in his legal capacity. In 1590 he arranged for his wife and several of his children to leave Paris rather than face the ordeal of the siege, but his wife fell into Spanish hands and had to pay 175 crowns to regain her freedom. In 1591 L'Estoile discovered that he was on a list of suspects drawn up by the fanatical Sixteen. In 1601, after peace had been restored, he sold his office to a certain Nicolas Martin, who cheated him. The result was an interminable lawsuit. At the end of his life L'Estoile had to raise money by selling his collection of medals. He died as a Catholic in 1611. L'Estoile's reputation rests on his diary. His political allegiance is unclear, and he admitted at the end of his life that he had some difficulty accepting the teachings and practices of the Catholic church. He was a Gallican who disliked the Catholic counter-reformation which he viewed as excessively Spanish or Italian in character. After 1598 he occasionally attended Protestant services at Charenton, and his circle of friends included both Catholics and Protestants. Though a royalist, he disliked the last Valois and Catherine de' Medici, but conceded that Henry III might have been 'a good king' in less troubled times. L'Estoile liked Henry IV and grieved over his assassination. L'Estoile's *Journal de Henri III* is a valuable historical source. It repeats much contemporary tittle-tattle and cites contemporary broadsheets and popular ditties. However, it must be used with caution, because L'Estoile was better informed about events in Paris than in the provinces. He may have given some of his accounts a satirical or humorous twist, but there is no denying the liveliness of his narrative. His description of Henry III's favourites, or 'mignons' is a good instance of his partisanship and style: 'These fine mignons had their hair perfumed, curled and recurled by artifice, and pulled up over their velvet bonnets as prostitutes like to do, and their ruffs of starched linen were half a foot long so that their heads above them resembled that of St John the Baptist on a platter.'

The Siege of Cambrai (October 1595). In 1595 Pedro Enriquez de Guzman, count of Fuentes, the newly appointed governor of the Spanish Netherlands, launched an offensive in northern France. After capturing La Capelle and Doullens, he rounded on Cambrai. Henry IV, who was in Lyon at the time, was determined to save the town at all costs, but he urgently needed men and money. He appealed to the Dutch United Provinces for armed assistance and to the Parlement of Paris to ratify his fiscal edicts, but their response was slow. The governor of Cambrai, Jean de Monluc, sieur de Balagny was unpopular with the inhabitants. As they grew tired of being bombarded by 70 Spanish cannon, they opened their gates to the enemy. Balagny retired to the citadel, but surrendered on 7 September. (Ann Ronan Picture Library)

# Ambroise Paré

Ambroise Paré (1517–90) was one of the leading surgeons of his day, and gained a great deal of practical experience tending the wounded on the battlefields of France. The son of an artisan of Laval, he was apprenticed to a barber-surgeon. In 16th-century France surgeons were accorded a far lower status than physicians, who were always university graduates. In 1537, after serving three years at the Hôtel-Dieu, the main hospital in Paris, Paré became an army surgeon. At the siege of Perpignan, in 1541, he treated successfully Charles de Cossé-Brissac, the future Marshal of France. Four years later, he published a work on treating the wounds caused by arquebuses and other firearms and, in 1549, another on mending fractured bones. As one of King Henry II's surgeons, he was sent to the siege of Metz. After being taken prisoner by the duke of Savoy, he cured the governor of Gravelines of a leg ulcer and was rewarded by being set free. In 1557 Paré witnessed the French defeat at Saint-Quentin. As surgeon

to King Charles IX, he was present at the battles of Dreux and Moncontour. At Dreux, he treated many noblemen and poor soldiers, including many Swiss. 'I treated fourteen of them in a single room', he wrote,' all wounded by pistol shots and by other diabolical firearms, and not one of them died'. Following his return to Paris, he found several noblemen who had retired there to have their wounds dressed. Paré has been described as the father of modern surgery. When amputating limbs, he preferred to seal arteries with ligatures rather than to cauterise them with a red hot iron (the old method). In addition to practising surgery, he continued to write and publish surgical treatises. In 1568 he ventured into the medical field by publishing a book on plague, small-pox, measles and leprosy. In 1573 he incurred much criticism for a book on the procreation of man and of monsters. The faculty of medicine of the university of Paris tried to have his books banned, perhaps on religious grounds – he was suspected of Protestant leanings. In 1573, as a widower, he married in the church of Saint-Séverin in

Paris and chose as the godmother to one of his children the duchesse de Nemours, who was a zealous Catholic. Paré never openly dissociated himself from the king's faith and remained on the royal pay-roll under Henry III. He died in December 1590.

## Jean de Léry

Jean de Léry (1534–1613) belonged to a modest Protestant family from Burgundy. He became a shoemaker and, in 1557, was one of 14 Calvinists sent to enlarge the colony which Villegagnon had established in Brazil. During his stay, which lasted until January 1558, he was able to observe the strange customs of the native Tupinamba Indians. After his return to France, he married (in May 1559) and in 1562 became a Calvinist minister, serving first at Nevers, then at La Charité. In May 1572 he took part in the synod of Nîmes. Later that year, he fled to Sancerre from a massacre of Protestants at La Charité, only to be caught up in a terrible siege which lasted from March to August 1573. He described the event in his *Histoire mémorable de la ville de Sancerre* (1574) in which the inhabitants are portrayed as God's

children besieged by the forces of evil. An instance of cannibalism in which parents were driven by hunger to eat their dead child reminded Léry of the cannibalism he had witnessed among the Brazilian Indians. 'Although I spent ten months among the American savages in Brazil,' he wrote, 'and have often seen them eat human flesh (for they eat their prisoners of war), yet I have never been so horrified as by this piteous sight, which as far as I know, has never been seen before in one of our French towns under siege.' His work became very popular, especially outside France, and was translated into German, Dutch and Latin. In 1578, after serving as a minister at Conches (Burgundy), Léry settled in Geneva, but in 1581 and 1582 he attended provincial synods in Burgundy. In 1578 he published his principal work, *Histoire d'un voyage faict en la terre du Brésil*, which went through six editions in the author's lifetime. In it, he praised the natural goodness of the natives as yet uncorrupted by Europeans, but his Calvinist faith obliged him paradoxically to condémn their existence as that of a 'damned people abandoned by God'. From 1589 Léry lived in the Pays de Vaud. He died in 1613.

# Henry IV's conversion

After 30 years of almost continuous warfare, the French people in the 1590s had good reason to desire peace. War was not wholly to blame for their troubles. A series of poor harvests, possibly due to climate change, led to a sharp rise in food prices and famine. As hunger set in, so did disease which the armies helped to spread. In addition to plague, there was influenza, smallpox and typhus. Wherever plague struck, the better-off people fled and urban activities like markets and fairs were suspended. Urban crime grew as municipal officials fled to the countryside. And war added to all this misery. Between 1589 and 1592, military engagements were most intense north of the Loire, especially in the Paris region. Towns ran into debt as they bolstered their defences, paid for troops and gave supplies to passing armies in the hope of averting pillage. Troop movements disrupted

food production, exacerbating shortages and forcing up prices. The hardships suffered by the peasants caused them to rebel. The most important of these risings was that of the *Croquants*, which began in 1593 and soon spread to much of western France. Some gatherings of armed peasants were very large. At La Boule, near Bourges, between 20,000 and 40,000 assembled in May 1594. Henry IV sympathised with them. He allegedly said that if he had not been born to inherit the crown, he would have been a *Croquant*. The peasant revolts of 1593–1594 helped to convince him of the urgent need to end the civil wars.

The main obstacle to peace remained the question of the succession to the throne following Henry III's assassination in 1589. Henri de Navarre had succeeded him as Henry IV, but many Catholics refused to recognise him on account of his Protestant faith. The League, as we have seen, had chosen the cardinal de Bourbon in his place. He took the name of Charles X, but was imprisoned in 1588 and died in May 1590. Finding a replacement acceptable to Catholics did not prove easy. A possible candidate was the cardinal de Vendôme, the fourth son of Louis prince de Condé. As he had never taken major orders, his supporters argued he could marry and have children.

CHARLES.
Cardinal de Bourbon Né a la Ferté sous Jouare le 22
Decembre 1523 mort a Fontenay le Comte le 9 may 1590.

Charles, cardinal de Bourbon (1523–1590), the so-called 'King of the League' Charles X. As a prince of the blood he was useful to Catherine de' Medici in her political intrigues. He officiated at the marriage of her daughter, Marguerite, with the Protestant leader, Henri de Navarre in August 1572. Under Henry III he supported the Catholic League and signed the treaty of Joinville with Spain, but in 1588 he was arrested by the king and imprisoned at Chinon. After Henry III's assassination, the League chose him as king in opposition to the Protestant Henry IV, but he was still in prison and remained there till his death in 1590. (AKG, Berlin)

After his coronation at Chartres on 27 February 1594, Henry IV prepared to conquer Paris, but the governor, Charles de Cossé-Brissac, and the mayor secretly arranged for two gates to be opened. In this engraving by Jean Le Clerc after N. Bollery, we see Henry IV on his way to attend mass at the cathedral of Notre-Dame after his peaceful entry into the capital on 22 March. The crowds lining the streets and sitting at open windows are giving him an enthusiastic welcome. (Roger-Viollet)

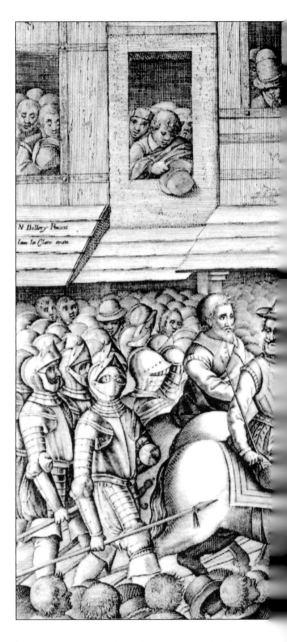

A group of Catholics, known as the 'Third Party', was formed to support him, but a rash attempt by the cardinal to win over pope Gregory XIV in March 1591 misfired badly. Meanwhile the pope angered Gallican opinion in France by excommunicating Henry IV and all his Catholic supporters. Another possible candidate for the throne was the marquis de Pons, Henry III's nephew. Yet another was Philip II's half-French daughter, the Infanta Isabella Clara Eugenia, but, as a woman, she was debarred from the throne by the Salic Law. The upshot of this genealogical tangle was that the Leaguers had no generally recognised candidate for the throne during the last four years of the war. Some could see advantages (particularly Spanish help) in supporting the Infanta's claim, but most French Catholics hated the idea. Many moderate Catholics were prepared to accept Henry IV if only he would give up his Protestant faith. They begged him to be 'instructed' in their faith, but for more than two years he wavered between doing so or strengthening his position by force. He needed to retain the support of Catholic loyalists without alienating the Huguenots. While procrastinating, he tried to balance the parties. He continued to rely on an inner circle of Huguenot advisers, but allowed Catholics to dominate the court. The royal chapel celebrated Mass each day and offered up prayers for the king's conversion.

In July 1591 Henry continued his balancing act by issuing the Edict of Nantes. This restated his willingness to undergo instruction once he had leisure to do so. At the same time it revoked the Edict of Union of 1588 and reinstated earlier edicts of pacification which had been more favourable to the Huguenots. Loyalist pressure on the

king to convert gathered momentum in the autumn when an assembly of the clergy, meeting at Chartres, decided to send a mission to the new pope, Innocent IX, informing him of the king's intention to be instructed as soon as possible. In January 1593 the Estates-General of the League met in Paris to decide who should succeed 'Charles X' on the throne. Despite strong opposition by some Leaguers, an invitation by Henry IV to joint talks was accepted by

a majority of deputies. The talks took place at Suresnes, near Paris. A truce of 10 days was agreed to allow negotiations to proceed. It soon emerged that the League's representatives, led by Pierre d'Épinac, archbishop of Lyon, would not challenge Henry's right to the throne, only his religion. On 17 May the leader of the royal delegation, Renaud de Beaune, archbishop of Bourges, announced that the king had decided to become a Catholic. This caused consternation among Leaguer extremists, but proposals submitted to the Estates by the duke of Feria in support of the Spanish Infanta's claim were rejected. The Estates declared that their laws and customs prevented them from choosing a foreigner as king. Henry IV, meanwhile, was receiving instruction in the Catholic faith, and on 25 July he solemnly abjured Protestantism in the abbey of Saint-Denis. Not everyone was convinced by his sincerity. An outspoken sceptic was the

The Edict of Nantes (13 April 1598). This was the last of a series of peace settlements between the French crown and the Huguenots. It did not establish a regime of religious toleration, as is often thought, but provided for the co-existence of the Catholic and Protestant faiths until such time as Catholic unity could be restored. Although the edict was more generous to the Huguenots than earlier settlements, they remained dissatisfied as they were not given equality with Catholics. The edict was revoked by Louis XIV in 1685. (Roger-Viollet)

preacher, Jean Boucher, who argued that Henry had been excommunicated by the pope and therefore remained a heretic. Normally the kings of France were crowned at Reims, but as that town was still held by the League, Henry was crowned at Chartres instead on 27 February 1594. In the ceremony he promised to expel all heretics from his kingdom. Many large towns now

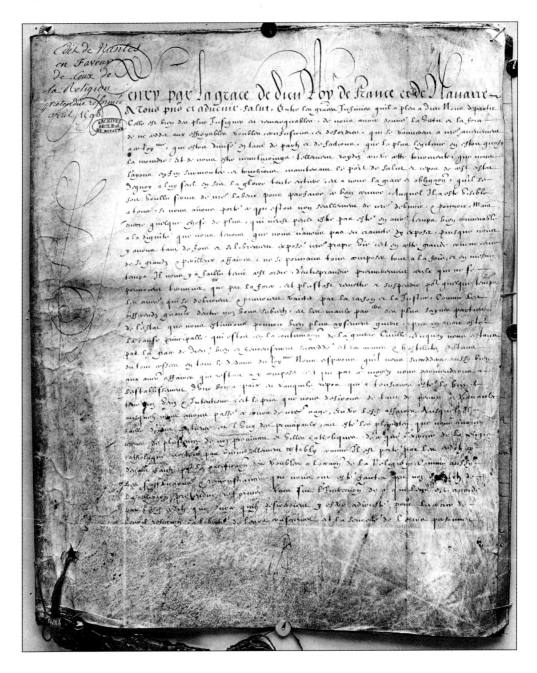

rallied to him, but in Paris he continued to be resisted by radical elements. Mayenne, however, had left the capital, and the governor, Charles de Cossé-Brissac, had been won over to the king. In March Cossé-Brissac plotted to hand Paris over to the king, and on 22 March royal forces converged on the capital from all sides except the south. Two of the city gates were opened from within and the chain barrier across the Seine was lifted. Meeting little resistance, the royal troops reached the city centre. At 6.00 am, Henry IV entered by the Porte Neuve and proceeded to Notre-Dame where he attended Mass. Afterwards, he lunched at the Louvre, then toured the streets amidst crowds shouting '*Vive le roi !*' At about 2.00 pm Henry watched the departure of the 3,000 Spanish troops who had garrisoned the city for the League. As he did so, he cried out to their commander, the duke of Feria: 'My compliments to your master, but do not come back!' About 120 Leaguers who refused to submit to the king were banished from the capital. In September 1595 Henry was absolved by Pope Clement VIII in return for certain promises. The submission of Paris encouraged other towns in France to do likewise. Some urban authorities found themselves under popular pressure to renounce the League. This was demanded, for example, by the weavers in Amiens and the wine-growers in Dijon. In Lyon, the people discarded their green Leaguer scarves for white royalist ones. A militia captain hoisted a large portrait of Henry IV outside the town hall and the city surrendered the next day. But not every town submitted without a struggle. Laon, for example, had to be conquered. The same was true of other towns in Picardy and Ile-de-France. Many towns made the king pay heavily for their submission. Town governors, in particular, were handsomely rewarded for their part in the process. Thus, Claude de la Châtre, governor of Berry, received 250,000 crowns for bringing Orléans and Bourges into the king's camp. Leaguers were often given offices at the expense of Huguenots, who had to be content with promises of

compensation. Sometimes Henry IV agreed to settle a town's debts, to remit its tax arrears or to exempt it from tax in the future. Huge sums were also paid to some individual noblemen. According to the king's finance minister, Sully, he disbursed between 30 and 32 million *livres* in treaties 'for the recovery of the kingdom'. Henry was accused of demeaning the monarchy by paying out such bribes, but, as he told Sully, he would have had to pay 10 times as much to achieve the same result by the sword.

Henry had secured Paris, but still faced several threats in late 1594. The League continued to oppose him in many parts of France, but he believed that without the active support of Spain, it would soon crumble. On 17 January 1595, therefore, he declared war on Spain. He aimed 'to lift the mask of religion' which his opponents were using as a cover for their resistance, to give himself the option of taking the war to Spanish soil, and to reassure the Protestant powers that his conversion had not turned him into a puppet of Spain. By declaring war on Spain, Henry IV transformed the civil war into a foreign war aimed at liberating France, and turned the Leaguers into traitors. The king was most concerned about the security of France's northern border, but he was also aware of the threat posed for Burgundy by the Spanish army in Italy. This materialised in May when a Spanish army, 10,000 strong, marched on Dijon to assist Mayenne who was still holding the citadel after losing the town to the royalists. Henry left Paris on 24 May and after rallying troops at Troyes, marched in haste to Dijon. On 5 June a small force of cavalry under Marshal Biron ran into the Spaniards near Fontaine-Française. At first, Biron thought they were only outriders, but he soon came to realise that he was up against the entire Spanish vanguard. Though heavily outnumbered, Henry IV led furious cavalry charges, forcing the enemy to withdraw. Fontaine-Française was only a minor battle, but its consequences were important. The Spanish commander, Velasco, refused to have anything more to do with the League after falling out with Mayenne, and without Spanish help the duke was unable to regain Dijon. On 22 September Henry signed the treaty of Lyon which effectively removed the Spanish threat from his eastern border. Mayenne was now little more than an isolated rebel, and Henry won over the people of Burgundy. Eventually Mayenne made his submission to the king, in return for the governorship of Ile-de-France and three security towns. Henry also took upon himself the settlement of the duke's war debts. The dukes of Épernon and Joyeuse soon followed Mayenne's example. As Guise had already joined the king in January, only the duc de Mercoeur among the great nobles remained obdurate.

Having more or less gained control of Burgundy, Henry IV needed urgently to attend to the defence of his northern border. In June 1595 a Spanish army under the count of Fuentes captured first Le Catelet, then Doullens, an important stronghold north of the Somme. From there, Fuentes moved against Cambrai. Writing from Lyon on 12 September, Henry announced that he would save Cambrai or die, but he was desperately short of funds. On 7 October the people of Cambrai opened their gates to the enemy. With a large army Henry IV laid siege to La Fère, the last Spanish outpost south of the Somme, but the campaign proved difficult and costly. In the spring of 1596 the Spaniards launched a new offensive. They captured Calais in April, then Ardres. In May, matters improved for Henry when La Fère at last capitulated. In March 1597 a force of Spaniards disguised as peasants captured Amiens in broad daylight. Henry IV was shattered by the news. He was desperately looking for new sources of funding and his predicament was worsened by the refusal of two Huguenot commanders, Bouillon and La Trémoïlle, to assist him with their troops. They even seized royal revenues in areas under their control. On 8 June Henry joined Biron, who had been besieging Amiens since April with only 3,000 men. The king brought with him sizeable reinforcements as well as artillery. By June he had thrown a series of forts linked by trenches around Amiens. The Spanish garrison

defending Amiens was numerically inferior to the king's forces. He could also count on the support of opponents of the League within the city. On 15 September a relieving army of 21,000 men, led by the Cardinal-Archduke Albert, arrived outside Amiens. While Henry was away hunting, Biron and Mayenne (now fighting for the king) beat off two successive attacks. As the cardinal withdrew, Amiens surrendered. On 25 September Henry IV entered the city in triumph and watched the departure of the Spanish garrison. The fall of Amiens sealed the fate of Mercoeur who had been holding out for the League in Brittany. Early in 1598 Henry set off for Brittany with an army 14,000 strong. As he approached, town after town expelled its Leaguer garrison. On 20 March Mercoeur came to terms with the king. He gave up the governorship of Brittany in return for the huge sum of 4,295,000 *livres*. He also agreed to marry his only daughter to Henry's bastard son.

Two settlements were needed to bring the war to an end, one with the Huguenots, the other with Spain. Both were achieved in 1598. In April, the Huguenots were induced, after much hard bargaining, to accept the Edict of Nantes. This generally confirmed the provisions of earlier edicts. Protestant worship was allowed on the estates of Huguenot nobles, at two places in each *bailliage* and where the Huguenots could prove that it had been openly practised in 1596 and 1597. Huguenots were allowed access to offices. Bi-partisan courts were to be set up in the parlements. But Huguenots were not allowed to raise taxes, to build fortifications, to levy troops or to hold political meetings. Secret clauses granted the Huguenots a limited degree of military and political independence. They were allowed to hold for eight years all the towns under their control in August 1597. The crown undertook to pay the garrisons.

In May 1598 Henry IV concluded the Treaty of Vervins with Spain. All towns captured by either side since the peace of Cateau-Cambrésis were to be returned. This meant France had to give back Cambrai, but she had recovered Calais and other places.

# Why did the wars take place?

Human motivation defies analysis. We cannot tell how many people in France took up arms purely in defence of their religion. Some undoubtedly did. They may have believed that Catholicism or Calvinism was the only true faith and that its preservation was essential to their personal salvation. Faith in the 16th century was stronger than it is in the western world today. It had not yet been undermined by the scientific revolution of the 18th century and modern materialism. Nor did anyone think in ecumenical terms. Truth was deemed indivisible, and heresy was generally held to be not just wrong belief, but also a social pollutant which could incur the wrath of God. A Protestant within a predominantly Catholic community, who set himself apart from society by refusing to take part in a religious procession, or to obey the church's law on fasting, seemed likely to bring down God's punishment on the community as a whole.

Not all the belligerents in the French Wars of Religion may have been as religiously committed. Some may have used religion as a pretext to seize a neighbour's property, to harm a business rival or to pay off a private score. Modern research on urban society in 16th-century France has uncovered many instances of such behaviour. Religious motives were often tangled up with mundane interests. Yet if religion was not the only cause of the wars, it remained a potent source of militancy. By 1562, when the first war broke out, France was already religiously divided and violence had become the norm as the crown tried to suppress dissent by force. The wars were but an extension of earlier martyrdoms and massacres. Another important factor was aristocratic discontent. In the absence of a large standing army or civil service, the king looked to the nobles to help him govern the kingdom. The old nobility, known as the 'nobility of the sword', provided the captains of the companies of heavy cavalry which were the flower of the army. Nobles had played a leading part in the Italian Wars. They also assisted the king to govern the provinces by serving him as governors or lieutenants-general. But the relationship between king and nobility was one of mutual dependence. If the king looked for service, the nobleman expected rewards for himself and his friends or clients in the form of offices or gifts of land or money. Exclusion from royal favour spelt ruin to a nobleman. Fighting was a way of life for many of them, and under strong kings, like Francis I or Henry II, they had been given many opportunities of displaying their martial virtues; but when a serious financial crisis forced Henry II to sign the Peace of Cateau-Cambrésis, bringing the Italian Wars to an end, many nobles felt they had lost their *raison d'être*. Some also resented the fact that the crown owed them wages.

When Henry II died in 1559 the kingdom was plunged into a grave constitutional crisis, because the king's successor was a mere boy. His mother, Catherine de' Medici, became the effective ruler. As a woman, she commanded less authority than a man and, as an Italian, she became a victim of popular xenophobia. She leant on members of the aristocratic house of Guise, thereby offending the Bourbons, who as princes of the royal blood, had a better claim to help the king to govern his realm. The Guises were foreigners by origin and championed Catholic orthodoxy, while the Bourbons were French and supported the Protestant Reformation. In this way aristocratic, religious and even nationalistic passions become engaged.

## Why did the wars last so long?

The main reason for the extended duration of the wars was the crown's inability to enforce a lasting settlement. It lacked the means to keep an army in the field for long enough, and many peace settlements had to be made prematurely. They were invariably too generous to one side or the other, and, as compromises, satisfied no one. They were bound to collapse and their unsatisfactory terms served only to fuel new conflicts – paradoxically, the failed settlements served to prolong the strife. Although the kings of France were envied for their fiscal powers by fellow monarchs, they were never able to cope with the rising cost of contemporary warfare. In the absence of a large standing army, the king had to hire foreign mercenaries, mainly German or Swiss, who insisted on being paid on the nail. Artillery was also very expensive, Numerous exemptions and anomalies prevented the French tax-system from satisfying the king's needs. He was accordingly forced to rely on expedients like the sale of offices or the alienation of parts of his domain. This brought him into conflict with the Parlement of Paris which had the duty of upholding the 'fundamental law' banning the practice. Seeking assistance abroad could be counter-productive, because loans needed to be repaid with interest. Every now and then the king had to stop fighting not because he had been defeated, but because he needed to replenish his empty coffers. Troops that were disbanded without being paid lived off the countryside and terrorised the peasantry. The religious wars spilt out all over the kingdom in acts of violence by mutinous troops. Desertion was a daily occurrence. By issuing edicts of pacification, the crown may have hoped to end the fighting, but it never intended to allow two religions to co-exist permanently in the kingdom. The aim was always to patch things up pending the restoration of religious unity. The setting up of security towns helped to fuel further conflicts by giving the Huguenots bases from which they could operate militarily and divert royal revenues into their own war-chests. The wars were also fuelled by individual, infamous acts of violence. The assassination of the duc de Guise in 1563 created a vendetta between the houses of Guise and Châtillon which lasted, regardless of peace settlements, until Coligny's murder in 1572. The Massacre of St Bartholomew threw more fuel on the flames of civil strife by destroying whatever credibility the Valois monarchs had retained among their Huguenot subjects. Although they did not reject monarchy for a republic, as some historians have suggested, they looked for theoretical justification of their armed resistance. Even regicide became an acceptable doctrine, which, working on fanatical minds, led to the assassinations of Henry III and Henry IV. Another event that prolonged the civil wars was the death of the duc d'Anjou in 1584 which created the prospect of a Protestant inheriting the throne of France. Confessional strife became bound up with royal legitimacy: could a Protestant, even one who converted to Catholicism, become king of France? The question caused bitter divisions within the Catholic and Protestant camps.

## The impact of the wars on France and her people

Two facts need to be taken into account when assessing the effects of the civil wars. Firstly, they were not continuous, but were punctuated by peaceful intermissions. Secondly, not all parts of France were affected equally. Some regions, like Normandy or Poitou, experienced much fighting; others, like Britanny, were largely spared. Yet the wars generally did cause serious hardship by disrupting normal economic activities. As peasants fled in terror from their homes, they abandoned their daily pursuits, and food production suffered in consequence. If a town was besieged, its economic activity was inevitably disrupted and, if taken by storm and sacked, it was put out of action for some considerable time. Yet the wars cannot be blamed for all the distress of the times. From about 1500 onwards the French population grew faster than food production, which was hampered partly by technological backwardness, partly by climatic changes. A harsh winter followed by a dry summer could wipe out a harvest; three successive bad harvests could cause famine which, in turn, would facilitate the spread of plague and other diseases. The winters of 1565, 1568, 1570 and 1573 were particularly harsh, and plague became more virulent, especially after 1577. Yet the population of France continued to grow. Some historians have argued that the wars did not affect its rise, but local statistics tell another story. For example, the population of Rouen fell by more than a quarter between 1562 and 1594 though this may have been due to emigration as much as death. Many Protestants fled to England or Geneva to avoid persecution. Some returned under Henry IV, when Rouen's population almost reverted to its pre-civil war level. Fighting alone cannot account for the death toll during the wars; famine and disease were also responsible. The total of deaths during the wars has been roughly estimated at between two and four million.

Constitutionally, the wars did terrible damage to the French monarchy, revealing its fundamental weaknesses. For all the monarchy's claims to absolute power, its effectiveness depended partly on the person of the monarch, partly on the support which he could expect from the nobility. By uncovering those weaknesses, particularly the inadequacies of the fiscal system, the wars pointed to the reforms that were implemented by Henry IV and his successors. In the longer term, the wars served to strengthen the monarchy by forcing it to adjust and reform.

## Did the wars solve the religious problem?

It is commonly assumed that the Edict of Nantes solved the religious problem in France by giving the Huguenots toleration and security. Nothing could be further from the truth. The edict's purpose was to create the conditions which in time would allow the kingdom to regain its traditional Catholic unity. By deliberately avoiding any mention of belief or doctrine it focused on the need to integrate the Huguenots socially into a Catholic state. The edict remained in force for 87 years, longer than any previous settlement, but relations between Catholics and Protestants were not peaceful during that period, because the edict was far from even-handed. Although Huguenots were given important concessions, they were denied equal status with Catholics. Their right of worship remained restricted, and the edict called for the restoration of Catholic worship in areas where the Huguenots had banned it. The latter were also expected to observe Catholic feast days and to pay the tithe. Denominational clashes continued to occur despite the edict. In 1611 trouble broke out between the regent, Marie de' Medici, and a Protestant assembly at Saumur. Cardinal Richelieu accused the delegates of 'disturbing the peace'. Following protests by representatives of the clergy at the Estates-General of 1614, King Louis XIII ordered Catholic worship to be restored in the small southern county of Béarn. When the local estates refused to do so, he led an army south and annexed Béarn and Navarre to France. In December 1620 an illegal Huguenot assembly at La Rochelle decided to resist the government by force. It ordered troops to be raised at public expense and divided France into eight military zones under the overall command of Henri de Rohan. In June 1621 Louis XIII led a crusade against the Huguenot rebels. The Peace of Montpellier (October 1622) confirmed the Edict of Nantes, but ordered the destruction of Huguenot fortifications, except at La Rochelle and  Montauban. Yet fighting soon broke out again, culminating in the siege of La Rochelle. The defenders eventually capitulated, and a new peace was signed. While confirming the basic text of the Edict of Nantes, the peace of Alès (June 1629) removed the Huguenots' hard-won political and military rights. Their rights of worship were acknowledged in theory by the state, but they were subjected to much intolerance until 1685, when Louis XIV finally revoked the Edict of Nantes, setting in motion a mass exodus of Huguenots from France.

# Further reading

Benedict, Philip,'The St. Bartholomew's massacres in the provinces', *Historical Journal*, 21 (1978), 201–25.

Benedict, Philip, *Rouen during the Wars of Religion* (Cambridge,1981)

Benedict, Philip, G. Marnef, H.van Nierop, and M.Venard (eds.) *Reformation, Revolt and Civil War in France and the Netherlands, 1555–1585* (Amsterdam, 1999)

Buisseret, D., *Henry IV* (London, 1984)

Carroll, Stuart, *Noble Power during the French Wars of Religion: the Guise Affinity and the Catholic Cause in Normandy* (Cambridge, 1998)

Carroll, Stuart,' The Guise affinity and popular protest during the Wars of Religion', *French History*, 9 (1995), 121–51

Constant, Jean-Marie, *La Ligue* (Paris, 1996)

Contamine, Philippe (ed.) *Histoire militaire de la France: 1. Des origines à 1715* (Paris, 1992)

Crouzet, Denis, *Les Guerriers de Dieu. La violence au temps des troubles de religion, vers 1525–vers 1610* , 2 vols. (Paris, 1990)

Diefendorf, Barbara B., *Beneath the Cross. Catholics and Huguenots in Sixteenth-Century Paris* (Oxford, 1991)

Greengrass, Mark,'Dissension in the provinces under Henry III, 1574–85' in *The Crown and Local Communities in England and France in the Fifteenth Century*, ed. J.R.L.Highfield and R. Jeffs (Gloucester, 1981), 162–82.

Greengrass, Mark,' The Sixteen: radical politics in Paris during the League', *History*, 69 (1984), 432–9.

Greengrass, Mark,'The later Wars of Religion in the French Midi' in *The European Crisis of the 1590s*, ed. P.Clark (London, 1985), 106–34.

Greengrass, Mark,' The *Sainte Union* in the provinces: the case of Toulouse', *Sixteenth-Century Journal*, 14 (1983), 469–96.

Greengrass, Mark, *France in the Age of Henry IV: The Struggle for Stability* (revised edn. London, 1995)

Hale, J.H., *War and Society in Renaissance Europe, 1460–1620* (London, 1985)

Hale, J.H., *Renaissance War Studies* (London, 1983)

Harding, R., *Anatomy of a Power Elite: The Provincial Governors of Early Modern France* (New Haven, Conn.,1978)

Holt, Mack P., *The Duke of Anjou and the Politique Struggle during the Wars of Religion* (Cambridge, 1986)

Holt, Mack P. *The French Wars of Religion, 1562–1629* (Cambridge, 1995)

Holt, Mack P., 'Putting religion back into the Wars of Religion', *French Historical Studies*, 18 (1993), 524–51.

Jouanna, Arlette, *Le devoir de révolte. La noblesse française et la gestation de l'état moderne, 1559–1661* (Paris, 1989)

Jouanna, Arlette, Jacqueline Boucher, Dominique Biloghi and Guy Le Thiec, *Histoire et dictionnaire des guerres de religion* (Paris, 1998)

Kettering, Sharon,' Clientage during the Wars of Religion', *Sixteenth Century Journal*, 20 (1989) , 221–39.

Kim, Seong-Hak, *Michel de L'Hôpital: The vision of a Reformist Chancellor during the French Religious Wars* (Kirksville, MO.,1997)

Kingdon, Robert M., *Geneva and the Coming of the Wars of Religion in France, 1555–1563* (Geneva, 1956)

Kingdon, R.M., *Geneva and the Consolidation of the French Protestant Movement, 1564–1572* (Geneva, 1967)

Knecht, R.J.,' The Sword and the Pen: Blaise de Monluc and his *Commentaires*' *Renaissance Studies*, 9 (1995), 104–18.

Knecht, R.J., *Catherine de' Medici* (London, 1998)

Knecht, R.J., *The French Civil Wars, 1562–98* (London, 2000)

Knecht, R.J., *The Rise and Fall of Renaissance France* (2nd. Edn., Oxford, 2001)

Le Roux, N.,'The Catholic nobility and political choice during the League, 1585–1594: the case of Claude de La Châtre', *French History*, 8 (1994), 34–50.

Lloyd, Howell A., *The Rouen Campaign, 1590–92: Politics, Warfare and the Early Modern State* (Oxford, 1973)

Lynn, J.A., 'Tactical evolution in the French army, 1560–1660' *French Historical Studies*, 14 (1985), 176–91.

Major, J. Russell,'Noble income, inflation and the Wars of Religion in France', *American Historical Review*, 86 (1981), 21–48.

MacCaffrey, W.T.,'The Newhaven Expedition, 1562–1563', *Historical Journal*, 40 (1997), 1–21.

Nicholls, D., ' Protestants, Catholics and Magistrates in Tours, 1562–1572': the making of a Catholic city during the Religious Wars', *French History*, 8 (1994), 14–33.

Oman, Charles, *A History of the Art of War in the Sixteenth Century* (London, 1937)

Parker, Geoffrey, *The Military Revolution: Military Innovation and the Rise of the West, 1500–1800* (Cambridge, 1988)

Potter, David, *The French Wars of Religion. Selected Documents* (London, 1997)

Potter, David,'Kingship in the Wars of Religion: the reputation of Henry III of France', *European Quarterly Review*, 25 (1995), 485–528.

Roberts, Penny, *A City in Conflict: Troyes during the Wars of Religion* (Manchester, 1996)

Roberts, Penny,' Religious conflict and the urban setting: Troyes during the French Wars of Religion', *French History*, 6 (1992), 259–78.

Roberts, Penny,'The most crucial battle of the Wars of Religion? The conflict over sites for Reformed worship in sixteenth-century France', *Archiv für Reformationsgeschichte*, 89 (1998), 292–311.

Roy, I., (ed.) *Blaise de Monluc. The Habsburg-Valois Wars and the French Wars of Religion* (London, 1971)

Salmon, J.H.M., *Society in Crisis: France in the Sixteenth Century* (London, 1975)

Shimizu, J., *Conflict of Loyalties. Politics and Religion in the career of Gaspard de Coligny, Admiral of France, 1519–1572* (Geneva, 1970)

Sutherland, Nicola M., *The Massacre of St. Bartholomew and the European Conflict, 1559–1572* (London, 1973)

Sutherland, Nicola M., *The Huguenot Struggle for Recognition* (New Haven, Conn., 1980)

Sutherland, Nicola M., *Princes, Politics and Religion, 1547–1589* (London, 1984)

Thompson, J.W., *The French Wars of Religion* (Chicago, 1909)

Wolfe, M., *The Conversion of Henry IV: Politics, Power and Religious Belief in Early Modern France* (Cambridge, Mass., 1993)

Wood, J.B.,' The decline of the nobility in sixteenth- and early seventeenth- century France: myth or reality?' *Journal of Modern History*, 48 (1976)

Wood, J.B.,'The Impact of the Wars of Religion: A View of France in 1581', *Sixteenth Century Journal*, 15 (1984), 131–68.

Wood, J.B., *The King's Army: Warfare, Soldiers and Society during the Wars of Religion in France, 1562–1576* (Cambridge, 1996)

Wood, J.B.,'The royal army during the early Wars of Religion, 1559–1576' in *Society and Institutions in Early Modern France Ed Holt, Mack. P* (Athens Georgia, 1991)

# Index

Figures in **bold** refer to illustrations

# Related titles & companion series from Osprey

## CAMPAIGN (CAM)
**Strategies, tactics and battle experiences
of opposing armies**

## WARRIOR (WAR)
**Motivation, training, combat experiences
and equipment of individual soldiers**

## ELITE (ELI)
**Uniforms, equipment, tactics and personalities
of troops and commanders**

## MEN-AT-ARMS (MAA)
**Uniforms, equipment, history
and organisation of troops**

## ORDER OF BATTLE (OOB)
**Unit-by-unit troop movements and
command strategies of major battles**
Contact us for more details – see below

## ESSENTIAL HISTORIES (ESS)
**Concise overviews of major wars
and theatres of war**
Contact us for more details – see below

## NEW VANGUARD (NVG)
**Design, development and operation
of the machinery of war**
Contact us for more details – see below

**To order any of these titles, or for more information on Osprey Publishing, contact:**
Osprey Direct (UK)   Tel: +44 (0)1933 443863   Fax: +44 (0)1933 443849   E-mail: info@ospreydirect.co.uk
Osprey Direct (USA) c/o MBI Publishing   Toll-free: 1 800 826 6600   Phone: 1 715 294 3345
Fax: 1 715 294 4448   E-mail: info@ospreydirectusa.com
**www.ospreypublishing.com**

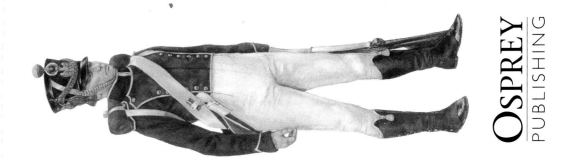

# FIND OUT MORE ABOUT OSPREY

❏ Please send me a FREE trial issue of Osprey Military Journal

❏ Please send me the latest listing of Osprey's publications

❏ I would like to subscribe to Osprey's e-mail newsletter

Title/rank _____

Name _____

Address _____

_____

_____

_____

Postcode/zip _____

State/country _____

E-mail _____

Which book did this card come from?

_____

❏ I am interested in military history

My preferred period of military history is _____

❏ I am interested in military aviation

My preferred period of military aviation is _____

I am interested in (please tick all that apply)

❏ general history    ❏ militaria    ❏ model making

❏ wargaming    ❏ re-enactment

Please send to:

**USA & Canada**:
Osprey Direct USA, c/o MBI Publishing,
PO Box 1, 729 Prospect Ave, Osceola, WI 54020, USA

**UK, Europe and rest of world**:
Osprey Direct UK, PO Box 140, Wellingborough,
Northants, NN8 2FA, United Kingdom

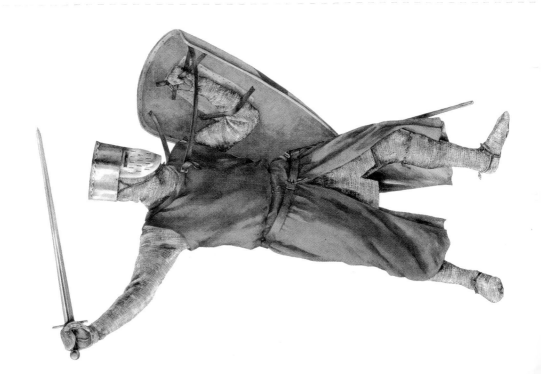

OSPREY
PUBLISHING

www.ospreypublishing.com

call our telephone hotline
for a free information pack

USA & Canada: 1-800-826-6600
UK, Europe and rest of world call:
+44 (0) 1933 443 863

**Young Guardsman**
Figure taken from *Warrior 22:*
*Imperial Guardsman 1799–1815*
Published by Osprey
Illustrated by Christa Hook

**Knight, c.1190**
Figure taken from *Warrior 1: Norman Knight 950 – 1204AD*
Published by Osprey
Illustrated by Christa Hook

POSTCARD